The Martin Management Method

About the Authors

Stephen Hawley ("Steve") Martin is Senior Partner and James Shannon ("Jim") Maxwell is Partner for Strategy Development of Hawley Martin Partners, a business consulting and branding firm that exists to help leaders take their companies or organizations to the next level. Steve was a principal and Senior Vice President of The Martin Agency during that firm's meteoric rise to national prominence.

Martin

A lifelong student of business as well as a strategic thinker and writer, he has authored 17 books, many on business management topics such as lean enterprise, lean manufacturing, product development, process based management and marketing communications. Jim worked with founder of The Martin Agency, the late David Martin, for ten years at Martin Branding as project manager on research and

Maxwell

branding studies. Jim has taught business courses at the University of Virginia and the University of Richmond. He is a graduate of the Jepson Leadership School of the University of Richmond, has a business degree from Virginia Commonwealth University, and a law degree from the University of Virginia. Send Steve or Jim an email if you would like to see how they might help your business or organization reach the next level.

Contact Steve at Stephen@HawleyMartin.com

Contact Jim at Jim@HawleyMartin.com

The Martin Management Method

by

Stephen Hawley Martin

and

James Shannon Maxwell

RICHMOND, VIRGINIA

CONTENTS

Our Story

Many people know my brother David and I took a small, local ad firm, founded as Martin & Woltz and renamed The Martin Agency, to national prominence. Before David and I, and other partners who joined along the way, sold it, The Martin Agency was cited as the "Hottest in the Southeast" by *ADWEEK* magazine. In May 2016 it was named "Ad Agency of the Year" for by one of the most prestigious organizations in the advertising business, The One Club of New York.

We learned a great deal growing that business, not the least of which is how other companies work. Or don't.

Nowadays, we put to work that knowledge to help other firms reach the top of industries in which they compete. And though we may be most widely known as advertising gurus, I can say with confidence it takes much more than smart advertising for a business to win.

Communications and branding are parts of the equation, of course. That's why we help organizations put a finger on a compelling identity, and why we develop ideas and communications for them that convey clearly what they stand for and offer. But our process goes farther to insure people within an organization embrace and live the vision we help our clients create. David wrote a book some years ago explaining how a vision is created entitled, *Be The Brand*. We still use that process today as an initial step, as Jim and I explain in Chapter One.

This book, however, goes into greater detail about what must happen after everyone has embraced the vision. They have to pull together with a sense of urgency to bring it into reality. We call the way to make that happen, "The Martin Management Method," or M3 for short.

What our method does is create a shared sensitivity, a sense of accountability and urgency in each of employee. Time and again the method has worked to get everyone pulling his or her own weight—perhaps even more than his or her own weight—and when that happens, and a clear vision exists, success is bound to follow.

The genesis of our method goes back a long way. I'll tell the story in brief. As a twenty-something ad executive, I'd just moved from Washington, D.C., to Richmond to partner with my brother in the newly named Martin Agency. Soon after my arrival, I joined the local chapter of the American Marketing Association for the same reason others join clubs made up of people in their line of work—to network and get to know others in order to make a name for myself and to attract business.

After a year or so, I ran for office and was elected vice president of programming, which meant I had to line up the monthly speakers. There were five or six vice presidents of this club, each covering a different area such as membership, fund raising, and special events. The way things got done was through meetings of these officers, which were called "directors' meetings." To keep these meetings running in an orderly fashion, Robert's Rules of Order was followed. At first I thought these Rules were kind of silly, but it wasn't long before I saw how they served a purpose. They assured orderly procedures were followed, and they resulted in consistency. A notebook was kept of all the minutes of every meeting. This notebook also held pertinent information concerning what each vice president did during the year such as a list of contact information for suppliers, and copies of invoices for items that had been purchased. This made a lot of sense. Every year the membership of the American Marketing Association changed somewhat. And every year the list of officers turned over, and a new president took the reins. People found themselves filling roles they knew very little about. But the club's purpose and direction and momentum continued because that notebook contained the information they needed to pick up where others had left off. In addition to the Rules of Order, the AMA also had a charter, bylaws, and written procedures. Without these, when new officers assumed their positions, it might have taken practically the whole year for them to get a handle on things.

At each meeting, the secretary kept minutes. These minutes served as a history and also helped keep everyone on their toes, because they were a public record of what the club had agreed to do. The only thing was, sometimes the minutes seemed to ramble, and often people didn't do what they were supposed to do because the secretary had failed to make it clear who had agreed to do what and when they had agreed to have it done. The president of the club often ended up doing most of the work—along with a few others who could be counted on to follow through.

The following year, I was elected president of the chapter, and the notebook was passed to me. I was happy for the exposure that came with the position, but I realized I probably was going to have to work like a beaver to get my day job done along with what was sure to come with this new position. After all, I had no authority over any of the other officers or members even though I had the title of president. Everyone in the group was a volunteer. Any could walk at any moment, or decide not to follow through on a commitment. I had no power over them, nor any recourse such as a performance review.

The first thing I did was change the way the minutes were kept. In our meetings at Martin we used action reports, which are similar to minutes except that they cut to the chase. They don't ramble on or recap a discussion, they report the decisions made and the actions to be taken. They clearly stated who has responsibility for the action and the deadline agreed upon to get it done.

Second, I didn't just stick these action reports* in the notebook to sit there until they were pulled out again and read at the next meeting, I sent a copy to all of the directors whether or not they'd been in attendance at the meeting, and I sent a copy to anyone else who might in any way be affected by the decisions which had been made.

I didn't stop there. Our chapter had a monthly newsletter and the president always wrote a column that appeared on the front page. I used that space to call attention to the people who had taken on different tasks, to give them a pat on the back for stepping up to the plate and committing to a specific date. I also praised those who had completed tasks already, or had made a special contribution.

And I didn't stop there. The president always opened the monthly luncheon meetings, so I used my time at the podium to say who was doing what and the deadline they were working toward. I'd ask them to stand to give them recognition. People like to hear their names, and they like the spotlight. I'm sure the exposure made them feel warm all over because

---

* You will see that we have renamed action reports "Action Registers" in the M^3 system.

they, like me, had joined the organization in order to meet people, to network, and to become better known in the marketing community of our city.

Now consider this. After all that exposure—once all their peers knew what they were supposed to accomplish—do you suppose any of those people dropped the ball? Of course not. If they had, whose reputation do you think would have suffered? Theirs, of course. If they wanted business from other members in a position to send it to them, they knew they had to demonstrate they could be counted on. The result was that year's volunteers not only followed through, they followed through in spades. They got more accomplished in more spectacular ways than had happened in anyone's memory.

Awards Were Used to Motivate

The chapter gave an award each year called the Golden Candlestick to the person seen as having gone above and beyond and contributed more than anyone else. As the year unfolded, I often lamented from the podium that I didn't see how we were going to choose just one recipient because so many had contributed so much.

This brings up another point. Awards can be a great way to call attention to people and get them working enthusiastically. My friend and former client Bill Monahan in his book, *Billion Dollar Turnaround*, writes about one he created called the "Top Performer's Award." Rather than just give bonuses and recognition to the sales force, he expanded this practice to include the rest of the company. Each year his primary team would choose top performers who had gone above and beyond what was expected in their jobs to achieve outstanding results. Everyone at Bill's company, Imation, had the opportunity to nominate whomever they felt was deserving. And rather than recognize only the winners, Bill also included spouses and partners, so the impact of what had been achieved would be felt within the family as well as by peers in the company. Recipients came from all functions, from every level of the business, and from other countries as well as the United States. A daytime meeting would be held of the entire headquarters staff, where coffee and ice cream or cake would be served. Winners would be flown in from wherever they lived and worked. There'd be a guest speaker, and the winners would then receive awards in front of this assembly. Announcements of the Top Performer Award winners were sent to hometown press and included in the company newsletter and on the web site. They included a photograph of each and rundown of accomplishments that had led to the award. This practice became so popular and generated such enthusiasm that business units in the different countries began having their own similar award programs in addition to the worldwide program.

Praise is More Powerful Than Money

I learned something valuable that year as president of the local chapter of the American Marketing Association. Praise is a powerful tool, often more powerful than money. Praise works because it makes people feel good. Money can't always buy that. And praise works for another reason. If everyone knows someone is supposed to complete a task—if all of their peers know because you praised them for taking it on—that person is almost surely going to do it, and do it well.

I have to say, my term as AMA president whizzed by. Things got done as they were supposed to. And you know what? Richmond won "Chapter of the Year" out of more than 140 chapters across the United States and Canada. It was the first time the Richmond Chapter had won, but not the last. And you know why? Everyone involved saw how to create a championship team. You can create one, too. You can reach the highest level of success and become the standout in your company or industry by following the process described in this book.

The process, by the way, has been refined and added to over the years to the point it now involves more than meetings, action reports, and praise. It has been fleshed out to a point it now can be instituted successfully in an organization as small as five people, or one that spans the globe. Those who have done so tell me that besides the thrill of victory that results from leading a winning organization, the biggest payoff is they won't have to work as hard as they did back before they learned how to get colleagues and employees to become accountable and motivated by a sense of urgency to get their jobs done. Read ahead, and my partner and I will explain how you can do this, too.

Stephen Hawley Martin
Senior Partner
Hawley Martin Partners

Talent wins games, but teamwork and intelligence win championships.

- Michael Jordan

Chapter One
Creating a Vision

This book is for anyone who wants to take a company, a department, a club or nonprofit, to the next level. It might be a business with as few as five people. It could be a service club, or it may even be a multinational corporation. As Steve mentioned in the Foreword, he used an early version to catapult the Richmond American Marketing Association to Chapter of the Year. David and Steve took a small, local ad agency to national prominence. One of our clients used it to turn around a business with 30,000 employees in offices on five continents. Whatever the case may be, it should start with a vision. Perhaps you have one already. If so, it needs to be communicated. People inside the organization must become sold on it and live it. People outside also need to become aware.

Tactics We Use to Communicate a Vision

TV/Radio/Print
Pod or Broadcasts
Public Relations
Events & Promos
Newsletters
Publications
Direct Mail
E-Mail Blasts
Books & eBooks
Billboards
Website

Social Media
Blogs & Blogging
Online Videos
Q&A Sites
Whitepapers
Referring Links
SEO - Organic & PPC
Comment Marketing
Webinars

If you do not have a vision firmly in mind, how can one be created?

We believe every person and every entity such as a business has something the person or entity can do better than anyone else. Just as every snowflake is different, each has a unique combination of talents and abilities. In the case of a company, what it is probably goes back to its beginning. Why did the founders create the company in the first place? What caused it to remain viable and in business to this point in time? The answers should provide a clue.

This unique ability is a person or a business's *raison d'etre*. It is the basis of a story that can be the springboard to greatness. Time and again we have found the path to success starts that way. It's what sets a company apart and gives it a core identity. When that identity is known, recognized front and center and practiced day in and day out by the leadership and staff of an organization, a powerful signal is sent to the world outside.

What's your story?

Can your story be summed up in a single word such as reliability? Safety? Variety? Fun? What does it all boil down to? That's the company's core identity. Its "One Thing."

Try this. Stroll down a hallway in your business and ask someone to give you a word that defines your company. You'll be fascinated by what you hear. And do not hear.

But if all you get are blank stares, take heart. A core identity exists. All organizations have their own unique story; it's just that sometimes what a company stands for and how that came about have been forgotten.

How to Put a Finger on the Vision

Start with a hard look inside the company. Use the questionnaire below and from the answers develop value propositions. Take these outside and talk with customers and prospects in order to connect and relate what has been found to the expectations and desires of the marketplace. Then bring what has been learned back inside and hold concensus groups among the business's leaders, stakeholders, and employees to create a vision everyone will buy into. The results can be powerful.

Ten Questions That Need Answers

1) Why do people like to work here?

2) What attracted you?

3) When someone outside hears the name mentioned, what do you suppose comes to mind?

4) What does this organization do better than any other?

5) Looking forward, what is it you wish to achieve?

6) What is the image or reputation today with key influencers?

7) What do you like most about what you do here?

8) Describe the ideal future:
   - What would it be like here 5 years from now if you could wave a magic wand and make it happen?
   - What must be done here for the organization to continue to exist and prosper into the future?

9) If in five years a major story about the organization about the firm appeared, what would you like the headline to say?

10) What do you believe to be the best single word to describe this organization and what it offers?

We have conducted identity studies among many leading firms and have found managers are often surprised to learn a powerful belief system has endured despite growth, mergers, or acquisitions. A corporate story spawns core beliefs, and core beliefs create an identity—that identity is your brand. That's why we encourage those leaders whose corporate stories we uncover to move quickly to reinforce that story and the identity it brings through indoctrination, training, communication, incentives, ratings and rewards.

What's in a name

Many business people do not truly understand what a brand is. They think it's a name or a logo. But not just any name or logo deserves to be called a brand.

A brand is a name or symbol or combination thereof that stands for something unique and desirable. A rose by any other name may smell as sweet, but a brand name and logo on a package will almost always command a higher price than a generic label.

A true brand creates an expectation of performance. It has value in and of itself. For example, when Rolls Royce Motors was sold, BMW paid 40 million British pounds ($65 million) just for the name and RR logo. Many in the automotive industry were aghast, believing that was quite a steal. Yet BMW did not get the rights to use the distinctive Rolls Royce grill or "Spirit of Ecstasy" mascot—integral components of the Rolls Royce brand. Without them a Rolls is hardly a Rolls.

Emotion needs to be the payoff

One of our specialties is bringing a brand to life through the communications we create. We have a special approach we use that's been around a long time, but most people never learned. It comes from Aristotle, who said that a speaker who is attempting to move people to thought or action must concern himself with pathos—their emotions. If the speaker touches only their minds, he is unlikely to move them to action. Aristotle believed, and we agree, that true motivations lie deep in the realm of passions. Let's be honest. Most of us use or manipulate facts to justify what our gut feelings [emotions] tell us we want.

How we breathe life into cold, hard facts

Think of an apple's glistening red exterior as the emotion. It's what people feel, see and react to when they choose one particular apple from the many on display in the produce section of a grocery store. Of course it doesn't occur to them on a conscious level, but the fruit under the skin—not the skin itself—is the real reason to eat the apple. The meat of the apple represents a product's attributes—the logical rather than emotional reasons to buy—its features and benefits.

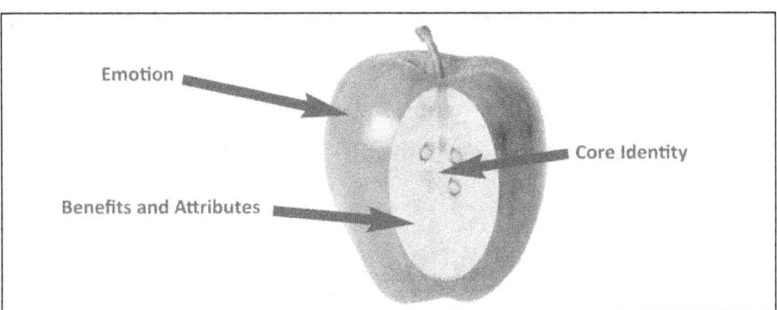

Emotion and identity are linked in a way that gives meaning, aura, mystique and value. For example, the core identity of Virginia as a travel destination is the state's wide variety of travel attractions, including mountains, beaches, history, and theme parks. So, "variety" might be the appropriate word to use in describing Virginia's identity with respect to travel. A long list of attractions gives people a logical reason to vacation in Virginia, but we would ask, "What emotion can be attached to it?"

Years ago, the Martin team came up with "Love," perhaps the strongest human emotion next to fear. We reasoned that Virginia is for mountain lovers, Virginia is for beach lovers, Virginia is for history lovers, and one Martin team member had the bright idea to drop the adjectives. The rest of the team agreed, and that's how "Virginia is for Lovers" came to be.

The rest is history. Before the campaign began running, Virginia enjoyed a great deal of repeat travel business, but this loyal cohort was growing old. Only 20% of the State's visitors fell into the much sought after young family market. In three short years following the campaign launch, the figure had grown to 35%, an increase of 75%.

Emotion (love), logic (lots to do), core identity (variety) inextricably linked. That's the underlying secret behind great and highly effective communications and what can create a compelling vision within your organization as the first step in getting everyone pulling together to bring that vision to reality.

Chapter Two
What's Wrong with How
Many Companies Are Managed

It's sad but true, teamwork is missing in many organizations. Imagine how well a business would run—how waste would be eliminated and things would hum along if everyone in a business felt important and that their contribution mattered. Imagine if they each felt a sense of ownership and responsibility. Imagine if only one level of performance was expected from everyone—the highest possible. Imagine if all men and women inside the walls of a company were considered to be of equal value, all integral members of the same team, and all in a position to make a vital contribution. Sure, someone has to play first base, and others the outfield. Someone must take on the grueling job of catcher, and whoever has the best arm needs to pitch. But each team member's goal is to be the very best at the job he or she has, every one of which is essential in its own way. And imagine that each person knows and realizes that only if they all pull together, each performing at the peak of his or her game, will they have a chance to win the pennant.

That's the kind of environment we would like to help you create. Among other things, we will challenge you to examine your team culture. Is it one of selective engagement, or is it one of collective accountability? Only by engaging your people through visible and personal accountability can you fully tap the full resources at your disposal.

Just about every organization keeps records and evaluates results, but rarely do their leaders build the kind of systems this book will lay out for you—systems that cause people to feel connected to the business, have clarity of communication and consistency of engagement. This sense of ownership usually does not exist because most leaders do not know how to bring it about. They do not realize a framework must be constructed to track and engage their people, not through the power of their personalities but through the integrity of their systems—systems that allow people to know instantly and continuously if they are winning or losing. Systems that provide a communication conduit employees can rely on to provide critical information. Systems that make performance tangible and visible and allow the leader to consistently elevate the intensity of engagement among all who are under the leader's supervision.

The leaders of virtually every business or organization we have worked with during the past twenty years have struggled to instill three intangible but important qualities in their people. They have strived to do so for good reason because— when the managers and employees of an organization possess them—the likelihood of achieving their vision is exponentially greater than it otherwise would be.

The qualities are:

• focus

• a sense of urgency

• visible and personal accountability.

You will agree, perhaps, that much of what people learn at seminars and through business books is conceptual. The concepts always sound good. What often is lacking, however, is a way to put the concepts into practice. Tools and systems that come together to form a complete process are needed.

We have found that focus is created when people throughout an organization understand whether the business is winning or losing. Unfortunately, this usually is not the case. Not long ago, for example, one of us at Hawley Martin was visiting a manufacturing business. He was being escorted on a tour and took the opportunity to speak with an individual working on a production line.

"I have a question for you," he said. "Right now, at this moment in time, is this production facility winning or losing as a business?"

The lady he was speaking to blinked. Then she replied, "Well, let me think. I've worked more overtime this year than I ever have before, so it must be winning. As far as I can tell, it's great."

When the tour arrived at the distribution center, our colleague stopped to speak with a forklift operator.

"Tell me something," he said. "Right now, at this location—can you tell me—is this business winning or losing?"

"Hummm," the man said. "I haven't seen my supervisor in the last three days. Typically, if things are not going well, I can't get rid of the guy. That leads me to believe everything must be okay."

These workers had no idea how the business was doing. Their answers were not business answers. Their only frame of reference was how things were going for them personally.

Ask yourself, would the people where you work know if the business was winning or losing if queried in this way?

Following a tour such as this one, the leaders of a business often give us a presentation that explains the business's strategies and goals. Typically, they also share information about how the business is doing. It is obvious the leaders are well aware of how things are going, but employees don't have a clue. Much time and energy is being spent at the top to direct the business and to measure results, but very little of that investment in time and energy is being translated to the people in the organization—people who could be helping or hurting a great deal when it comes to achieving objectives.

As this book unfolds we will go into detail about how to change this and involve everyone in the quest to realize the vision, but before we do it's important to understand that what most people think of as "leadership" simply will not deliver sustained focus, urgency and accountability on its own.

Why Conventional Leadership Is Not Enough

Most of us learned a type of leadership that is predicated on three Ps:

- Managing by Position,
- Managing by Proximity, and
- Managing by Persuasion.

We do not dispute that managing by these three methods can work—to a degree. Many companies have been driven to the top by leaders who practiced and institutionalized what we call, "managing by personality." This sort of leadership can indeed achieve results, but the results are almost always fleeting because they are dependent upon the leader and his or her being present. When the leader is not there, when the leader goes on vacation, takes a business trip, retires, or is relocated to another area of the business, his or her organization will usually flounder until someone else, who is also able to manage by personality, takes the leader's place.

Managing by Position

Leaders can be powerful people. In formal structures, their power is conveyed through title and authority. In other words, if someone has the title of supervisor, manager, director, vice president, president, CEO or some other such designation, authority has been bestowed on the leader by virtue of the position he or she occupies.

Traditionally, leaders use their titles and authority to achieve results. They set policy, give direction and make decisions that others are expected to execute.

Titles and authority are not bad. Every organization has them. But if the organization defines its leadership in terms of position and authority, rather than systems and processes, then it will not be able to sustain success over the long haul. The reason is that each of the three ways of managing by personality relies on a single factor—the individual leader. Remove the leader from the equation and the catalyst that drives performance has been removed—with the result that the team's performance often atrophies, flounders and may even disintegrate to the point of failure.

Management by Proximity

Ask yourself this. What happens when a high-level executive comes into a work area? Do employees work harder or more diligently? Does small talk stop and activity increase?

Of course it does.

It is perfectly normal for people to want to impress the one in charge. When the leader comes around in most organizations, people tend to work harder. Human nature is such that people want to look good, even if the "work" they are doing is little more than a command performance for someone they want to impress.

Proximity is directly linked to confidence. Leaders who feel connected, who are "tied in" to the workforce, often use proximity as a catalyst. In other words, when they are close to their employees their confidence is high, and they extract a strong degree of focus, urgency and accountability from the people they employ.

But, when the leader is not in the workplace for whatever reason, that influence diminishes in relation to the distance he or she is from the workplace.

Some leaders relish the experience of seeing work activity speed up when they are near their employees. It gives their egos a boost. They claim their frequent visits to work areas are part of "managing by walking around," a technique described in a popular business management book published some years ago, and they justify their actions by pointing to the higher productivity that results.

There is nothing wrong a manager walking around the workplace. It allows him or her to see firsthand what needs to be done, and it helps connect the manager with the workforce. But when it is relied upon to get better performance from employees and is the only way to know what they are doing, it is what we call "managing by proximity," a form of managing by personality. The sheer power of the manager's personality is what has influenced employees to perform at a higher level. Their performance is not connected to business necessity or a shared sense of purpose, nor do they perform out of a sense of accountability for what needs to be done to make the organization successful.

Performance by proximity is short-termed and is sustained only as long as a manager is visible within the organization. Performance resulting from a sense of accountability and a focus on goal achievement, on the other hand, is long-lasting. It will happen with or without a particular manager's presence. This is what you will soon be able to achieve.

Management by Persuasion

In recent years, the concept of involving others in decisions that affect them has found its way into the workplace. Industrial psychologists have brought this about by urging leaders to work toward increased employee involvement, participation, and empowerment. They have persuaded leaders that it's important to keep everyone feeling happy and contented, and to do so they need to obtain buy-in on decisions that affect them. To the detriment of many companies, this emphasis on attitudes has moved organizations away from a focus on the business of the business—away from an emphasis on getting the work done.

Employee involvement aimed at changing attitudes to

achieve an end result is actually a kind of persuasion. We agree that employee involvement per se is not bad—on the contrary, it is good. Certainly, it is a huge improvement over authoritarian decision-making. However, changing attitudes by building consensus takes significant time and energy that could well be better spent if a system were in place to guide decision-making and ground every person to a common point of view based on the answer to the question, "Are we winning or losing?" Without knowing that, and basing decisions and actions on the answer, how can everyone be expected move ahead with a shared sense of purpose. It would be as though everyone was a player in a baseball or football game in which no one knew the score. They would simply be going through the motions, which is the case in many companies today.

The Limitations of the "Three Ps"

We often come in contact with managers who use the three Ps to lead their organizations. Many do so with a fair amount of success. We think of such individuals as "Heroic Leaders" who swoop in with their red capes flying to get the job done. Often this happens when things are not going well and something must be done to turn around the situation.

Many who operate this way tell us it is simply easier just to do it themselves or to hand it off to one of a few trusted high performers to follow through. The problem is, the few helpers a leader trusts—if there are any—usually can only do so much, and the leader has a limited amount of time as well. Often, such leaders spend an inordinate amount of time putting out fires with the result that some things that deserve their attention simply do not receive much, if any, until they rise to the urgent-priority level.

We encounter many in this situation. Take Hannah, for example, a manager at a large information technology provider. Each day she arrives at her office to find no less than 35 or 40 emails, many displaying big, red exclamation points signifying something urgent needing her attention. On top of these newly surfaced problems, she's scheduled to have a monthly meeting with her staff. As the day unfolds, more urgent emails arrive along with issues to address her boss has delegated that are not actually in her primary area of responsibility. When the time comes for her staff meeting, she may take a few long, slow breaths to keep from hyperventilating and cancel the meeting in an effort to buy 30 minutes to devote to the many crises du jour.

There's a better way. Instead of expending energy using the three Ps to engage her team, it is much easier and more effective to have a system that does the persuading and gets employees engaged.

Our system calls for scorecards that show employees the status of their work relative to overall business goals, such as quality, safety, cost, productivity, people, and customer service. When employees see the scorecard, they know immediately why they need to perform because they see their work's connection to the organization's goals.

Our system also includes non-negotiables, which are minimum processes all leaders and teams need to adhere to if they are to remain consistent, focused and accountable. Leaders learn how to define, document and deploy key processes around goals, people, and systems—processes that form a non-nego-tiable way of working. In this way, the Martin Management Method creates an organizational framework that results in habit, discipline and structure, which in turn creates and sus-tains a sense of urgency and a clear and concise business focus—while driving a sense of collective accountability.

Where are you today with respect to realizing your vision? Are you moving forward? Happy with the progress you have been making?

Perhaps you feel you've been going around in circles, not getting very far. If so, it's time now to start in a new direction.

Chapter Three
M^3 Overview

Say you've identified the vision, and leaders and staff have bought in. Now it's time to use M^3 to get them moving toward it with a sense of urgency.

Without structure and guidance, the efforts and actions of leaders and workers within an organization can be chaotic, much as we imagine might be the case for a team without a playbook—whose players do not know the rules of the game. Its members might work hard, may try their best, but their efforts may do very little to advance the team toward the goal because they haven't been coordinated, choreographed or channeled in a way that gets everyone doing his part to move the ball forward. That is what M^3 is designed to do.

M^3 can be described as a methodology comprised of a few simple rules and actions involving scorecards, action registers, and interlocking teams. Once instituted, individuals will know what they need to do to succeed personally, as well as what they should do to help the organization succeed as an enterprise.

Like a playbook, M^3 consists of activities and rules intended to result in predictable outcomes, i.e., to move a company toward the accomplishment of its mission and the realization of a shared vision. Like a team that has studied its playbook and knows each play by heart, everyone in the organization works within clearly defined and commonly understood parameters. This gets the whole group working together like a championship team on a drive to the end zone.

Rather than the traditional corporate pyramid, M^3 calls for interlocking teams

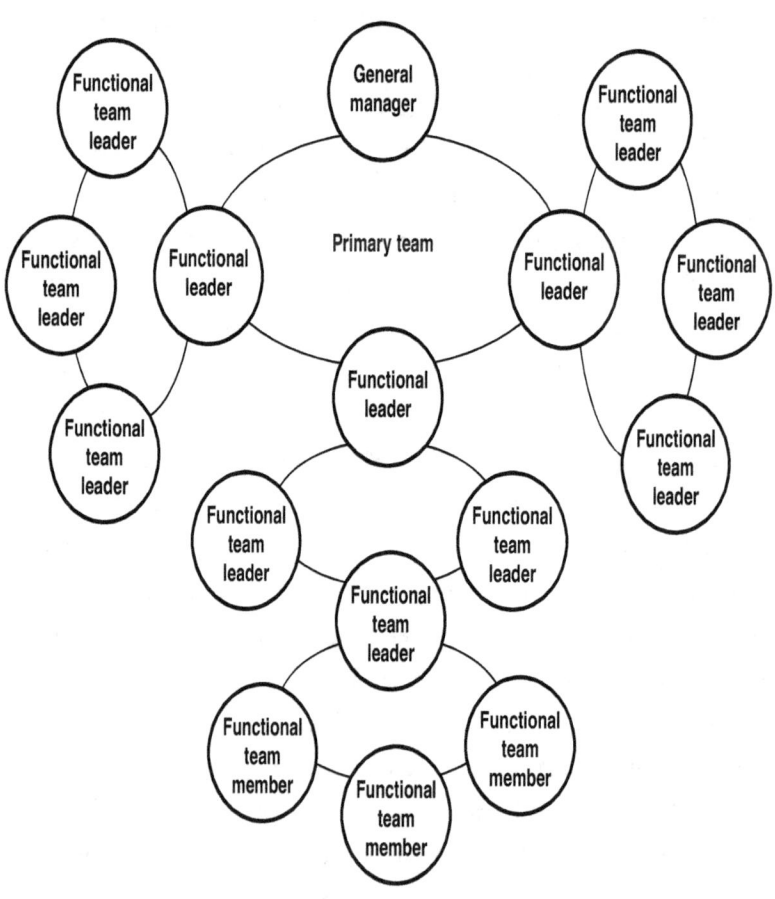

It's Important to Establish Patterns

Managing by personality creates an inconsistent workplace. People never know what to expect. Managing by process, on the other hand, drives consistency. Influential and effective leaders are often characterized as being consistent. They have a strategy, they stay the course, they know how to get there. They stay constant, stable and unwavering. Consistency starts with clearly communicating expectations and the consequences for failing to meet them. We call these non-negotiables.

Non-negotiables (rules) represent minimum requirements all leaders and teams throughout the company must adhere to in order to stay focused and consistent. For example, members of an organization using our method must attend certain meetings at regular intervals, they must be on time, and they must follow certain rules such as Roberts Rules of Order. Leaders should know and adhere to what team members expect of them and vice versa. Team members should know and adhere to what they expect of one another.

If you have ever been on a successful sports team, you know that everyone comes to understand what's expected of

---

Teams and Team Meetings

As a non-negotiable process, all employees belong to and participate on a team, which meets regularly, usually weekly. All team meetings use a crisp, consistent agenda that includes a review of scorecards, discussion of problem areas, and pass-up and pass-down information. Using the same agenda assures consistent information flow.

---

one another over time, and that no one wants to let down his teammates. Rather than wait for this to happen, each team in an organization should define behavioral expectations at the outset, i.e., what the leader expects of the team and what the team expects from the leader. Team members should also define what they expect from each other.

Team members and the leader define and document their expectations, then discuss them. Teams reach agreement on the visible behaviors defined by each expectation and commit to do their best to demonstrate them in daily operations. These are documented in a team handbook developed and written by the team.

Non-negotiables are combined with specific tools such as scorecards and action registers, which we are about to explain, to create a sense of urgency and accountability. They are part of a

---

The Team handbook

One method of achieving consistency is to "rule" by the book, the team handbook. This a document prepared by the team that:

- Gives order to meetings by spelling out the agenda.

- Gives a business focus to work by documenting the business scorecard and action registers.

- Outlines procedures for work done in the department.

- Serves as a history of performance (through the action registers).

---

process that gives a team and its leader to ability to identify the actions needed to move the organization toward specific goals.

A Communications System

Some reading this book will use our system to run a large company or organization. Others may use it to run a single department or a small business of less than a dozen employees. Communication will not be a big issue for the latter, but it's an ever-present challenge in an organization made up of hundreds or even thousands of people. Our method provides a way for the leadership of a large organization to communicate quickly and effectively and to coordinate efforts and activities of teams up, down and throughout the business.

This is possible because the organization's teams interlock so that communication can flow freely from one team to another. Many individuals will be on a team they lead, and these same leaders will be a member of a team on the next level up.

For example, the head of manufacturing at an industrial plant might be the leader of a team made up of the leaders of each production line team. But he or she will also be a member of the primary team headed by the plant manager—along with peer team leaders from engineering, marketing, material supply, and other disciplines that operate from the plant. In this way, what happens or is decided in a primary team meeting can flow quickly to the manufacturing group and to the other areas of the business through the team leaders of each.

Any number of teams can exist within an organization, starting with the primary team, which is headed by the top leader in the business and his or her direct reports. The team structure then cascades throughout the organization at all levels and functions.

Business Scorecards

Business scorecards, which will be discussed in depth in chapters four and five, are a key component of the system. They represent a simple and concise tracking mechanism that allows a team to monitor and respond to business metrics. The purpose of scorecards is to provide a clear and concise business focus for each team and to drive the direct lines of accountability for each team's contribution to the overall effort.

Business Scorecards

Scorecards give consistency to the communication process because they use a common language and appearance. All teams "speak" the language of achieving goals for production, quality, customer service, safety, cost and people.

The primary team should take on the task of developing a global scorecard to measure the overall performance of the organization. The global scorecard should address each important area of the business. Objectives should be high-level and supported by objectives incorporated on scorecards at other levels of the organization. This is how the leadership team is able to get everyone and everything moving toward accomplishing the organization's performance goals.

Once the global scorecard is complete, teams down the line should begin developing scorecards specifically defining how they support the global scorecard. Each team should have a minimum of one objective for each key business-focus area. Scorecard development cascades throughout all organizational levels until every team in the organization has its own set.

The primary team should review the global scorecard weekly during its team meeting. Teams in the rest of the organization should review their scorecards weekly as well, and they should review the global scorecard at least monthly.

Discussing scorecards gives meetings a sense of urgency. A scorecard also reinforces accountability. First, it does so by listing performance targets for each objective. As objectives are tracked, results are compared against these targets to gauge team performance. A scorecard also drives accountability because it identifies the owners of specific objectives. Owners track and update the metrics related to their objectives but are not necessarily the ones assigned to take corrective action when corrective action is required. Any member of the team may volunteer or be assigned to perform such a task when needed.

Teams are required to send scorecards monthly to senior management for review along with corrective action plans for any objectives not being met. Knowing senior management is going to review what you have or have not accomplished is highly motivational.

Action Registers

Action registers form another important component of M^3 because they make accountability on the part of employees visible and measurable. It's one thing to tell someone he is accountable for an action. It's another for someone to know his action, or lack of action, will be seen and noted by his peers as well as upper management.

The Action Register

An action register is a logical extension of the business scorecard. It is the primary tool driving accountability throughout the organization by publicly documenting the assignment of tasks to specific individuals, dates for completion of tasks, and results. Every team must create, monitor and use an action register. Leaders can also use action registers to create and track personal accountability.

Action registers document action items that result from team meetings. An action register, for example, details corrective action plans the team and its members need to take to improve performance metrics that are not meeting targeted levels. Meetings begin with an action register review of items that should have been completed for that meeting and conclude with an action register review of new items identified during the meeting. This includes verbal and written verification of the persons responsible and the agreed upon completion dates.

In summary, our system is a combination of non-negotiables, scorecards, action registers, and interlocking teams. These form a powerful process comprised of systems that will enable you to fully harness the collective power of the people who make up your organization. The Martin Method enables you to mold them into an all-star team that's pushing in unison toward goals you have set.

In upcoming chapters we will detail the specifics of the system and its implementation.

M³ Overview

Every member of the organization is on a team. In large organizations teams interlock to facilitate communication and the coordination of efforts to support organizational goals.

- The primary team creates and maintains a scorecard based on the mission, goals and vision of the organization.

- Each team creates and maintains a scorecard with objectives that support the primary team scorecard.

- Every team holds a regularly scheduled meeting, preferably once each week.

- Every team must create and use an action register that documents the corrective actions being taken on scorecard items that have fallen below target, as well as noting who is taking the actions and when they are due.

Chapter Four
Scorecard Overview

Business scorecards are an integral component of our system because they are repositories of an organization's goals—the key destination points on the corporate journey to greatness. An important feature of scorecards is that they can be brought together from each area of an organization to form a picture of what is going on throughout the business at any point in time. Having this picture in focus helps leaders make the critical and timely decisions needed for success.

Focusing on more than one or two areas of the business will be required if company-wide improvement is the goal. The task might be compared to that of a Little League baseball coach who is trying to build a better team. He needs to do what he can to improve every aspect of the game he possibly can—the pitching, hitting and fielding of the young players who make up his team. To overlook any one of these three major areas could be what brings about a losing season.

Each business area has a number of activities that affect its overall performance—just as in baseball. Under hitting, for example, there would be different things to work on such as hitting curve balls, fastballs and change up pitches. Fielding would, among other things, include handling ground balls, flies, throws from the outfield to the cutoff man, and throwing the ball from third to first base.

Each player has different metrics he needs to work on, depending on his position. The catcher has to worry about getting the ball from home to second on a steal. The short stop has to think about handling a short hop and the accuracy and speed of his throw to first. All these activities combine to produce a winning or a losing team based on how well they are performed. It is the same in a business organization.

What's most important in your organization? Communication? A way to gauge performance fairly and accurately? Accountability? Most leaders tell us each of these is important. They find it difficult to rank them in order. That's why all three have been linked together through the scorecard.

A Balanced Approach Is Best

We find that those primary team leaders who take a balanced approach to goals and scorecards tend to achieve the best results. The top-level scorecard should focus on **strategic goals.** For these to be accomplished, the key is for the lower level teams to identify and focus on **tactical objectives** that support each strategic goal. In this way, everyone in the organization becomes engaged in support of the strategic vision and corporate mission.

Perhaps you already have a scorecard system. If so, ask yourself if works like a thermometer or a thermostat. When someone looks at a thermostat, he or she sees the current temperature. That may be interesting, but what is more useful is one that works like a thermostat. If things are too hot, a thermostat controls air conditioning system to bring the temperature down. If the temperature is too cold, it will switch on the furnace to raise the temperature. That's how our system is designed to work.

Scorecards Help Drive Accountability

A business scorecard immediately shows employees the status of their work relative to overall business goals, such as quality, safety, cost, productivity, people and customer service. When an employee looks at his team's scorecard, he should immediately know why he needs to perform because he can see how his work and the work of his team connects to the organization's goals. We suggest using scorecards that are color-coded (red for underperforming, green for on target). Anyone using M^3 will know within five seconds of looking at a scorecard whether or not the team is winning or losing.

Scorecards Educate, Facilitate and Motivate

The scorecard should give guidance about what's important and why it is important. It should reinforce the value of winning and the consequences of losing. For example, when a scorecard is part of a system. it will help educate employees more so than one that's posted on a bulletin board where people can choose to look at it, or ignore it. People actually have to interact with a scorecard with metrics on it that relate to their area and level of the business. These are metrics they can impact, control and be held accountable for.

A scorecard should facilitate. It should start by setting the tone of the weekly team meeting. If the scorecard is updated with progress or lack of progress toward goals prior to the team meeting and is visually projected during the meeting so that everyone can see it, it will get everyone focused on what needs to be done, and who is winning and who is losing. Green items trigger recognition of accomplishments; red items trigger discussion, problem solving. Once plans are made on what needs to be done, they need to be documented in the action register with specific names and target dates for completion.

When a scorecard is linked to a way to identify who is accountable, it motivates people to get a job done. Without scorecards and action registers, leadership will have to revert to the 3 Ps (power, persuasion, and proximity, i.e., managing by personality) to engage employees and cajole them to perform. In other words, management may unnecessarily have to devote more time, energy and attention to a situation the team would be addressing.

Scorecards Convert Strategy into Action

As a leader of your organization, you have no doubt spent a good deal of time and effort developing a vision and path to reach it. Scorecards can insure you are on the path, making progress because they allow the leadership team to see what is happening in each area and throughout the organization. When a company's leaders know whether income is down or up, they know how the company is doing overall. But seeing the components of income such as quality, safety, costs, customer feedback and employee retention, can tell leaders what is happening on a deeper level. It may even help you see around corners. For example, if all the various components are improving, but the company's earnings are declining, external factors may be overwhelming the company's efforts. Conversely, if earnings are up and the various components are down, it is probably only a matter of time before earnings begin to decline.

Scorecards do not take the place of an accounting system, but they do give leaders an important tool to use to take corrective action in order to drive results. Because they enable leaders to see where particular metrics are headed, they offer warning signs that indicate action needs to be taken before green turns to red.

Scorecards can help leaders balance priorities. By establishing a few key metrics that link directly to corporate objectives, leaders can avoid metric overload and focus on those that will drive the business where they want it to go. This aligns employee behaviors with corporate objectives.

In the next chapter we will begin to look at the specifics of developing effective scorecards.

Chapter Five
Goals Can Lead to Success

A large, family-owned business we know of ran into trouble because the owners had a habit of not sharing information with employees. After a particularly good year, the owners decided to give every employee a 13-inch flat screen television.

The Best Buy truck brought them to the loading dock, and this delivery was followed by a big Christmas lunch. The company president stood at a podium and called each employee up one by one and presented each with a TV.

Within two hours the president was beside himself with anger and frustration.

Since the employees of this company had no firsthand knowledge of how the company had actually performed that year, they could only speculate based on how they personally felt. And how most of them felt was that they had worked harder that year than they had ever worked in their lives, and all they got to show for it was a lousy 13-inch TV.

Couldn't it have at least been a 32-inch model?

What this illustrates is that in the absence of business knowledge, what is left is individual perspective, and individual perspective can be very dangerous because an entitlement mentality is often the result. When an individual operates in a vacuum, he or she is likely to calculate what he believes is owed him, and the calculation may bear no relationship to reality.

This underscores the need companies and teams have to be working toward visible and tangible goals because, at the very least, this shifts peoples' focus away from themselves and on to the business of the business. As we have said and will say many times in this book, people need to know at all times whether they are winning or losing. This is what will move them away from the personal entitlement mentality so prevalent in most companies today.

Scorecards can accomplish this because they make a company and a team's goals visible.

Potential Key Focus Areas

Quality, Innovation, People, Finance, Safety, Productivity, Efficiency

---

Key Focus Areas

One of the first questions to be addressed, then, is goal setting. Goals need to relate to key focus areas of the business.

Key focus areas sometimes go by different names such as themes, buckets, priorities. They typically cover such things as costs, quality, innovation, people, finance, safety, productivity, and efficiency. These key focus areas should come from the vision or the mission of the organization. If the vision or mission is well written and thought out, the themes should be embedded in it.

One way to create a scorecard is to set it up using and Excel Spreadsheet. The key focus areas appear in the first column of the scorecard. Each team throughout the organization should have at least one metric that ties to each focus area. No cherry picking is allowed. The goal is to drive connectivity through common focus areas and the scorecard format, which should be the same throughout the organization. If the leader were to walk into any team throughout the organization, for example, and ask what that team is doing to support "People" or "Efficiency," for example, he should instantly get an answer.

The next column is for SMART Objectives. SMART is an acronym that stands for Specific, Measurable, Obtainable, Relevant, and Timely. The team needs to help develop and agree to what they are going to measure and work toward improving. This, of course, needs to be specific to a team's role and area of the business as they relate to the key focus areas selected by the primary leadership team.

The "Target" column is used to state the thresholds of red and green, i.e., whether the team is winning or losing in the area. Some companies also use yellow and other colors to denote transitional areas. This may make sense and be helpful in mature systems, but when starting out, we recommend that only red and green be used.

The next column shows the name of the person who owns the key focus area. This individual populates the scorecard within the frequency defined as non-negotiable. One company we know populates metrics every seven days. In this company, the owner is obligated to populate the scorecard by close of business on Friday at 5 o'clock eastern time, no matter in which time zone the owner may reside.

Ownership of Goals

The owners' names appear in the owner column. We do not believe groups or teams should be designated as owners.

Business Scorecard

Key Business Focus Area	SMART Objective	Target	Owner	Tracking Frequency Visible Indicator					Comments
				8/3	8/10	8/17	8/24	8/31	

48

It is important that owners be physically present in meetings. If a single individual is not responsible for the data and its accuracy, it will become possible to sidetrack discussion from what is going to be done about a red metric to whether or not the data is indeed accurate. Whether or not the owner actually gathers the data him or herself, that person needs to be able to speak to and defend it. That way, all a company CEO has to do is look to the left to see who is responsible. He should be able to pick up the phone or email that person to ask the status of an objective at any given moment. We suggest leaders actually do this from time to time so that every person who owns an objective will take the system seriously.

Frequency of Data Population

In a perfect world, scorecards would be updated every seven days and meetings would take place weekly. Of course, this may not always be possible. Metrics of a strategic nature, such as some that may be found at the top executive level, may only be available on a monthly basis. Even so, most teams should meet at least once a week. We recommend this because we believe it is important to *build an operational rhythm that fosters a performance habit*. In situations where updated metrics cannot be made available weekly, one or more persons on the team can usually predict what the numbers are likely to be. Corrective actions can then be identified and taken to head off the anticipated slip in performance.

Watch Out for Unintended Consequences

In choosing metrics, leaders and teams need to be sure to

consider what behavior a particular metric will drive. If only quality is being measured, for example, a factory can probably make the highest quality product of its type ever made—but it may cost a fortune. If only cost is being measured, no doubt costs can be cut, but the company may end up producing a poor quality product.

Often, metrics are selected because the persons doing the selecting want them to be green. They want to look good. The question must be asked, was the metric selected because it's easy to achieve? Make sure it provides useful results.

Are there too many metrics? Having too many causes confusion and too many things to focus on. Every metric does not have to be on a scorecard. Only the most important should be. If a small number of metrics are selected, they will be what the team will focus on. If a team has eight metrics, for example, it shouldn't have a problem focusing on that many each week. If the team has 25 metrics, it will probably be able to focus on ten at most. The team will probably end up focusing on those that are easiest to handle and achieve, and these may not be the most important.

The Phenomenon of Goal Creep

Even though we recommend that 15 or fewer SMART objectives be tracked by each team, we have seen that teams, particularly on higher levels of an organization, often load up scorecards with many more. This may happen due to what we call "goal creep." This takes place because those on the higher-level do not have confidence that an effective process is in place at the lower level to improve a metric. As a result, the higher-level team members may decide to track the metric themselves. This can backfire. Because the members of that team are watching the metric, it is almost certain they eventually will be tempted to take actions to improve it. Once they do, it will not be long before they own the objective.

Where Does a Metric Belong?

As was implicit in the previous discussion, it's important to identify and place the right metric at the right level of the organization. Obviously, responsibility for a metric needs to be placed where it can best be impacted and controlled. When we work with an organization and discover metrics on a scorecard that belong at lower level, we have usually found a clue that a system is not in place to link together scorecards at the various levels. It should be the job of leaders and teams on the higher levels do this.

To determine where a metric belongs, the question to ask is whether the individuals at a level are in position to take direct action to affect the metric, or must they enlist the help of others at a different level either above or below them.

It's also important to understand that the types of metrics are different at different levels of an organization. They typically become more basic at lower levels, and of course, there must be accurate data available for a metric to be tracked. If leadership wants to track an inquiry conversion rate, for example, there must be a way to do so. If there isn't a way at present, how difficult will it be to put a system in place and is it worth it?

The journey must be worth the climb.

When Good Enough Is Enough

It's important not to let perfection stand in the way of "good enough." Often metrics can be obtained that are good enough to provide an early indicator as to whether the organization is on track to meet goals. We often see concern that the numbers available to a team are slightly off, that the team may have to wait for accounting to close the books before a totally accurate number will be available. In cases such as this, it is usually more helpful to have an early indicator than it is to have perfection. It may be possible to improve the metric's accuracy over time, but that should not stop a team or a leader from getting started.

In practice, most scorecards go through many different iterations as time goes by. A scorecard system ought to be viewed as a living organism that can be improved upon, updated and changed as a situation or resources change.

The important thing is to move ahead. Even if a scorecard isn't perfect, putting it into practice will likely bring more and better results than waiting to have something that is. Early on, scorecards will need updating more frequently than when a system has matured. The first update may come in three months. Then it may be six months before another update makes sense. Then a year. In any case, it makes sense to consider updating scorecards at least annually.

Chapter Six
Creating Scorecards

Scorecards throughout an organization should follow the same format, look the same, and the same language should communicate whether a business is winning or losing. For example, it should be possible for someone from an organization to walk into any team meeting in the building, or into that company's offices in Seattle, Miami or Montreal, look at the scorecard projected on the screen and immediately be able to read and understand it.

Cascading Scorecards

What we call the Global Scorecard is the top scorecard in an enterprise that has deployed M^3. This could be the scorecard used by the senior management team of a global company. It could be the one used by a plant manager, or perhaps the senior manager of a single division of a company. It could be the management team of a small business. Whatever the case may be, it is the scorecard for the highest-level team using the process.

Supporting the Global Scorecard are Local Scorecards built by the teams that are going to use them. Everyone on a team needs to be involved and have input on this so they all buy-in.

Recently, one of us was working with a company that did not do this. The vice president of operations decided to take it upon himself to develop scorecards for every team throughout the organization. After all, he told us, he had worked his way up from the bottom and knew all there was to know about each area of the business. So he took a weekend and built the global scorecard for operations, each plant manager's scorecard, every departmental manager's, and each one all the way down to the shop floor.

The goals he came up with were probably 95 percent on target with respect to what the different teams would have come up with on their own. The problem, of course, was that the teams did not own the scorecards he had built because they had not been part of the process.

Let us add that it may be all right and even desirable for management to make suggestions, and in some cases even to mandate how certain metrics will be tracked such as safety or quality. The vice president's mistake was not involving or consulting the individuals under him.

The What, Why and How of Scorecards

Non-negotiables or rules give organizations the "what" and the "why." The "what" is that each team has to have a scorecard, it has to be in a predetermined format, and it must tie to particular focus areas identified by the primary team. The answer to "why" is that everyone needs to support and be working toward accomplishing the corporate vision.

Once everyone understands what needs to be done and why, it is up to the individual teams to determine **how.** How will each team make the system work? For the system to work, the scorecards need to be built locally. To insure they support the Global Scorecard as intended, they need to be approved by the team at the next level up.

Setting Targets

Obviously, targets need to be realistic. You may be far from where you would like to be with respect to a particular metric, but it doesn't make sense to try to eat the elephant all at once. If world class is 99 percent and we are now at 75 percent, it would not make sense to set the goal at 99 knowing we will not be able to reach that goal for more than a year. A *glide path* needs to be established by setting milestones. Perhaps the goal for the first three months might be to move from 75 to 80. Once reached, the goal might be to move from 80 to 85 and so forth. Goals need to be achievable while moving the organization in the right direction.

Also, when starting out, we recommend all metrics be given the same weight. But as time goes by and the system evolves, it may make sense for this to change because it will likely be the case that some metrics are more important than others.

Scorecard Iterations

We've found that on average most scorecards go through six iterations before goals are identified that clearly tell a team whether it is winning or losing. This happens for several reasons. As teams work with metrics they typically learn to break them down into components that can be impacted in ways that influence the business. This is one way scorecards help to educate their users. People learn to focus on the component or components that truly drive the overall result. A scorecard needs to be revised to take advantage of what has been learned.

Sometimes a scorecard will need to be revised because individuals had pet concerns they wanted included that have turned out not to be particularly relevant. Often, though, it has to do with whether or not it's possible to obtain the data needed to track a metric. The group may come up with something they would like to know that would help monitor progress toward an objective only to find that actually mining the data simply isn't practical or feasible. For this reason, it is important to look upon developing scorecards as an ongoing, evolving process. Once a goal has been reached or is no longer relevant for whatever reason, it should no longer be necessary to track it.

Revising Goals Upward

Suppose an area stays green and never goes into the red? It will probably make sense to revise the goal by elevating it to a more ambitious level. In fact, we recommend that a metric be reviewed with such a revision in mind if it has remained green for 90 days or more. It's likely either the goal as been accomplished and should be changed or deleted, or the green threshold should be raised. This is an opportunity to motivate continuous improvement.

Scorecard Development Summary

As already discussed, the senior team sets the key focus areas based on the organization's mission and vision and develops the global scorecard. Once the global scorecard is available, each team should come together and brainstorm how it can support the key focus areas. We recommend that if at all possible each team should identify at least three objectives under each area.

Once this has been done, the scorecard should be submitted up one level for approval. This higher-level team should scrutinize each objective to confirm it will indeed support the key focus area to which it is assigned. Once this is accomplished, and the scorecard is approved, the team can begin tracking.

Once a quarter, the senior team should look at all the scorecards to make sure there are no conflicts, that specific objectives are at the right levels and that everything works together to support the overall mission. We also recommend that each team make a presentation of its scorecard and action plans to the senior team at least twice a year.

Chapter Seven
Making People Accountable

Most leaders would do whatever is necessary, within reason, to place themselves in the enviable position of leading workers who possess a keen sense of personal accountability. No doubt these leaders imagine how easily tasks would get done and how quickly goals could be accomplished. They would no longer having to worry, follow up, or cajole.

We find, however, that in most organizations a majority of leaders think that day will never come. Often, they end up doing the work that others should be doing for themselves because this seems easier than lighting the fire required to compel those workers to do it for themselves. If the leaders stopped to think about it, they would realize this course of action is counterproductive. But in the heat of the moment, they often don't have time to think long term and follow the path of least resistance.

It's easy to fall into the trap of "doing for" others. A colleague of ours tells a story to illustrate just how easy. It has to do with his two sons, ages 10 and 12, who love to play sports—especially baseball.

Back when we played baseball, a player had two things: a bat and a glove. But nowadays there's a lot more equipment—different gloves depending on the position, metal bats of different sizes and weights, wood bats, catcher's gear, batting helmets. So our colleague bought bags to hold his boys' equipment.

Last spring, during baseball season, he used to drive the boys to practice on Saturday mornings. At nine o'clock, they would be standing by the car, sipping Gatorade, and waiting. Before our friend would climb into the car, he would check the bags to make sure everything the boys might need was there.

Often it was not.

So he got in the habit of taking an inventory, seeing what was missing, which was usually half their stuff, and tearing through the house to find the errant items. Because the coach had a rule that players who were late had to run laps no matter who was at fault—parents or boys, he'd have to race to the field at breakneck speed to get them there by 8:59.

One day, halfway through the season, the boys blew the horn while our colleague was searching for their gear.

The car was in the garage and the sound reverberated throughout the house. His brow furrowed, and his face flushed red. A puff of smoke exited his ears. He calmly walked to the car and told the boys in an even tone to go and find their own stuff.

Our friend realized something important that day. He had gotten into the habit of "doing for" the boys, and they had come to expect it. He had created a culture of dependency, rather than one of accountability. The responsibility for what had happened rested squarely on his shoulders, but it wasn't too late to reverse the situation.

When he and his boys got to the field, the coach stopped our colleague and said, "You and your boys are usually on time. Something unusual must have happened."

He could see the coach was about to let the boys off the

hook, just as a boss might let an employee off who is usually dependable. By this time, however, our colleague had realized what he should have recalled long before. Consequences must be enforced or people will come to believe the powers that be aren't serious. He told the coach the boys needed to run.

And run they did.

Creating Accountability

It goes without saying that a sense of personal accountability is essential on the part of managers and staff if an organization is to achieve a high level of performance. Fortunately, there is a way to create a sense of personal accountability on the part of everyone. It's done by making who is accountable for a given task visible for all to see. An Action Register is the tool.

How Action Registers are used in meetings to create accountability among team members will be discussed later. But an Action Register does not have to be just a meeting tool. It can be used as well on a one-on-one basis to make people accountable outside of meetings. One company we know of, for example, had a serious problem because workers had stopped taking personal responsibility. The situation was turned around using personal Action Registers—as the following actual case history illustrates.

Some years ago, the CEO of a company we worked with had read a book on the topic of creating a great place to work. He decided he wanted to create a culture in which people would feel that his company, too, was a great place to work.

The CEO arranged a visit to the company's primary manufacturing facility. The factory was shut down early on the afternoon of his visit. Everyone was given a t-shirt that said the company was going to be a "GPTW" (Great Place To Work) at a company barbecue for employees and their families.

A few days following the barbecue, the CEO unveiled his plan to the company's management. This included using flip charts, which were handed out to each manager. The flip chart had a statement printed at the top that said, "What Can I Do to Make You Believe This Company Is Committed to Becoming a Great Place to Work?"

The managers were told to get their staff together once a month for a meeting at which this chart would be used. The idea was to create a dialog with workers that would lead to the delivery of the promise.

A front line supervisor at this company has a span of control of about fifty people. The supervisor would pull these people together once a month, stand before them with the flip chart and ask the question, "What can I do to make this a great place to work?"

The result was a disaster. Imagine what these workers came up with. Here is one example:

"I have lower back issues and the chair I have to sit in all day exacerbates the problem. I've done some research and found one that should help me come to believe this a great place to work, provided you get it for me. It's called the Arrow Chair, and it sells for only $1800. Here's a printout about it from the OfficeMax Web site, along with the model number."

Multiply this by fifty and you will have a glimpse of what the supervisor now had to deal with. It wasn't long before the flipchart meetings and the efforts of management to create a great place to work had resulted in a culture of dependency. Employees came to expect the managers at to do their bidding, rather than vice versa. The managers were told making employees happy was part of the job. Before long, they had so much on their plates not much business was getting done.

As you might suspect, it wasn't too long before the CEO who'd had this brainstorm was gone. The question then became, "How do we turn the situation around?"

First, the monthly 'wish list' meetings were cancelled. But that alone wasn't enough. The culture of dependency continued. Leaders would arrive to work with a manageable list of what they needed to get done that day. As a manager would walk into the building, one of his employees would come up to him with a problem. To show how this would work, let's call the employee "David" and the manager "Sam."

David might say, "Uh, Sam, my paycheck was wrong this week. I worked four hours of overtime on Sunday and didn't get paid for it."

Sam was conditioned to say, "No problem, David. I'll take care of it," and one more thing would be added to his list. Because of the monster the GPTW program had created, by the time Sam arrived at his office a few yards down the hall, he was likely to have added six more items to his ever-burgeoning list. The situation seemed hopeless.

But there was a way to fix it. Accountability had to be made personal and visible. This was accomplished through the creation and use of personal action registers. Each manager was given a pad of them and instructed on their use.

The personal action register consisted of a white top

sheet and a yellow second sheet that became a copy. Let's have David and Sam put on a demonstration to show how the personal action register works.

David sees Sam coming in from the parking lot. "Oh Sam, my paycheck was wrong this week. I worked four hours over-time on Sunday and didn't get paid for it."

Sam pulls out the personal action register. "Let me be sure I understand," Sam says. "You worked four hours overtime on Sunday, and when you got your check this week, it was short the amount you should have been paid for the Sunday over-time, is that correct?"

"That's right," David says.

"First, let me say I'm sorry that happened, David. It appears a mistake was made and needs to be straightened out. The person who handles payroll is Linda Johnson in account-ing. She's just down the hall, third door on the right. I want you to see Linda by five o'clock, today," Sam says as he fills out the personal action register. "I'm going to circle back to you today at five to make sure you and Linda got this straight. Here's your copy of this action register. I'll keep the yellow as a record of our conversation."

In this exchange, Sam practiced active listening by repeat-ing back to David what David had told him, and Sam legit-imized the issue by telling David he was sorry it happened. Sam also got clarity about both the issue and what David needed to do about it. Sam did this by putting it in writing so there could be no dispute. If Sam had not, it is quite possible David would plead ignorance later on. Also, Sam made a com-mitment to David. He made it clear he would come to see him at five o'clock. It was important for David to follow up on that commitment.

When Sam sees David at five o'clock, one of two things will have happened. Either David will have seen Linda and resolved the matter, or he will not. If David did, that's the end of the story. Sam will then be able to close out the action register and file the form in Sam's personnel file.

But let's say Sam gets back to David and asks how it went, and David says, "It didn't."

"I'm sorry, what do you mean, it didn't?"

"I mean, I was in here on Sunday, put in four hours of work, and company didn't hold up its end of the bargain. It was not my error. It was the company's error, and I want my money."

Sam will then say, "Is there anything else you would like to say about this?"

"Just that I was wronged, and I want my money."

"Well, David, I am sorry you feel that way, but the path to your money is not through me. The path to your money is the one I gave you earlier. Linda is the person who can help. But since you feel as you do, I'm going to give you an extension until tomorrow at five o'clock. I'll check with you then to see if you have reconsidered. I hope you have a great evening."

At five o'clock the next day, Sam needs to see David. Of Course, it's possible David may not have done anything, once again. David may be angry, but Sam should not give in. Sam needs to stick to his guns, and he needs to be backed solidly up by management above him. If David goes over Sam's head to Sam's supervisor, and Sam's supervisor sides with David, the entire action register system will crumble, fall apart, and that will be the end of it. If David continues to stonewall, the yellow sheet needs go into David's personnel file. In this way, Sam will have will begin to accumulate documentation on a problematic employee whose days at the company are likely to be numbered. The yellow sheet will be used as an exhibit Sam can produce along with others when the day arrives for David's next performance review.

Assuming they adhere to this system, Sam and his peers in management eventually will find they are using fewer and fewer personal action registers. At some point, workers will get the message. They will realize that if they go to a boss and ask the boss to do what they are able to do for themselves, the boss is going to pull out an action register pad. They are going to realize it's a waste of time to ask the boss to do what they can do themselves.

When this is understood, people will begin to do things for themselves. Teaching people to do things for themselves is to empower them. You may recall the aphorism, "Give a man a fish and you will feed him for a day, but teach a man to fish and you will feed him for a lifetime."

The problem many leaders have that deters them from putting this into practice is that they worry about hurting other's feelings. These leaders should ask, did the man feel bad, angry or sad about having to fish for himself, rather than have a fish handed to him? He may well have felt bad or angry or disappointed at first. He may not have liked it at all until it dawned on him he now had the knowledge and power to feed himself and his family. This shows that feelings and empowerment often have very little to do with one another.

Empowerment or no empowerment, some leaders will no doubt feel uneasy about implementing this approach. They simply do not want employees to be unhappy. Leaders want those in their charge to feel good about the company and their supervisors. Let us say, this is perfectly normal—most leaders would. Nevertheless, we submit that when it comes to business, bottom line results are what matter most. Certainly, results are what shareholders and stakeholders at all levels of the business expect. If the choice is between winning or having employees feel good, winning is the right selection. Winning will benefit everyone in the long run, including whichever employee may happen to feel unhappy at a given moment in time.

Let us quickly add, however, that the personal action register pad is not for every company. In the case of the company just described things had gotten so bad there was probably no other way to turn around the situation. Whether you decide to use this or not, you may want to ask yourself what you are doing to make accountability personal and visible.

As indicated above, how people feel in the short run is less important than what people do that enhances performance in the long run. So the important and relevant question to ask is whether the actions and activities that take place as a result of a company's policy move the business forward. If so, the policy is good for the company and the people the company employs. The danger is that without the appropriate policy, thoughts and actions will revolve around how people feel rather than what they do, and that can kill performance. If something is not done, the organization will almost certainly fall short of achieving the level of performance it is capable of.

Chapter Eight
Teams and Team Member Performance

Many so called high performance systems have come along in the past ten or fifteen years such as Lean, ISO, Green Belts, Six Sigma, 5S and others. These systems were often implemented and sustained through the three Ps (Proximity, Persuasion, Position) discussed in Chapter Two.

Performance Today
Often Implemented and Sustained Through
Proximity, Persuasion, Position

- ISO
- Lean
- Green Belts
- Six Sigma
- 5S
- Command Centers / Production
- Boards
- High Performance Teams

Whether or not you have been exposed to one or more of the systems, we have found that practically every business in American has exposed its managers to team training. Teams have been thought to be the key to eliminating the corporate pyramid hierarchy in order to build a more streamlined and efficient organization. Empowered teams were said to push decision making closer to the issues that need to be addressed and into the hands of those most familiar with the issues— who should presumably be able to find the best solutions. Organizing into teams, in other words, has been thought to be the way to build a high performance organization.

Properly implemented, teams can certainly do all that. But in many if not most cases, they have not. What has been missing is that most organizations today are driven not my collective accountability but by selective engagement, and this doesn't help create effective teams.

The truth is most companies think they have teams, but in reality they do not. They have what they call teams, of course, but when the first layer of the onion is peeled away, what is exposed is a leader and his or her staff—not a team in the true sense of the word.

Let's look at an example of such a so-called team. The leader's name is Charlie. On his team is probably at least one individual who is Charlie's "go to" person. We will call him Ralph. Ralph shares the leader's values, his work ethic and belief system. The two go way back. When vacation time rolls around, Charlie will be certain not to schedule his and Ralph's vacation at the same time.

Let's think about how things work in this set up. Perhaps it has been a bad day. All kinds of issues have arisen—high absenteeism, goals were not met, several customers are upset and need attention or hand-holding. Just about everything that could have gone wrong, did go wrong.

Charlie goes to Ralph and says, "Could you stay after work today for 30 minutes and let's brainstorm some ideas and build an action plan so that tomorrow we can get things back on track."

What is Ralph going to say? He will say, "Yes," of course. He is ready to stay as long as necessary because that is the way Ralph is.

Then there is someone else on Charlie's so-called team, we will call him Harvey, who is the absolute opposite of Ralph. If Charlie were to go to Harvey and ask if he could stay after work, Harvey would probably say, "I'm sorry, but I have a life outside this place. I've got other things to do."

Harvey is the type of employee who should be on an employee improvement plan, he should be monitored and counseled, but from Charlie's point of view, taking on Harvey's makeover is low priority. Charlie has goals to meet, customers to please and metrics he's responsible for that are in bad shape and need attention. He simply has too much on his plate already.

Charlie lies awake at night worrying about Ralph. Charlie knows how important Ralph is to him, that he gives him much more than a fair share of the work to do. What if Ralph becomes fed up with all the work being piled on him, sends out his resume, gets a job offer and leaves? That would be a nightmare. Charlie would give Ralph a raise to price him out of the market if he could, but Charlie's hands are tied. Because of the anemic economy, the funds simply are not there. So Charlie decides he needs to think twice before he gives Ralph more assignments. The next one could be the one too many that pushes him out the door. So Charlie comes to the conclusion the only avenue open to him is to do whatever comes up next himself.

Many managers today are in the same situation. They take the attitude, "It's easier, faster, more simple for me to do it myself."

What is wrong with this?

In the first place, it's not fair to Charlie. He already has more than he can handle. He's already close to being burned out. If he keeps taking on everything himself, he is almost certain to reach a breaking point. So what is Charlie to do? How can he build an effective team?

Performance Today
The Current State of Leadership

- Reliance on the 3P's: Leaders influencing through their defined Position, Proximity, and powers of Persuasion

- Many leaders "Manage by Personality." Good intentions drive cultures of dependency, not accountability

- True high performance teams rarely exist as most teams are driven by selective engagement, not collective accountability

- No shortage of continuous improvement programs, but the operating system to sustain them is non-existent

- Metrics today represent Thermometers, not Thermostats

- No Leadership Legacy – Organizational changes create vacuums and voids

- Employees at all levels looking to leaders to provide an operating environment where there is Clarity, Connectivity, and Consistency

---

Building an Effective Team

It's important at the outset, or in Charlie's case if he wants to change things, for the members of a team get together and to discuss and agree on how they will work together. For this to happen, these three questions must be answered:

What does the leader expect of the team?

What does the team expect of the leader?

What do the team members expect of each other?

The leader needs to put down on paper what he expects of the team. These should be in the form of statements about what the team members should do. For example, rather than something non-specific such as, "be available or responsive," the leader ought to put down something specific and measurable such as, "return phone calls or emails within four hours."

The leader might say, "I want my team members to tell me bad news as soon as they hear it. I don't want them to wait until the next meeting."

Team members need to put down in writing what they expect of the leader and of one another. For example, the team probably expects its members to support each other in every way—as in all for one and one for all. In other words, they probably expect each member to do his fair share of the work and not to try to shove it off on someone else.

The non-negotiable expectations decided and agreed upon should not be personality-based. They should be operational so that if a new leader comes in to run the team, he or she will be able to review the non-negotiables and pick up right where the former leader left off. Moreover, team expectations and non-negotiables should be written up, signed by all, and kept in a team handbook. When new members join the team, they need to be made aware of the expectations and they be required to sign off on them as well.

Once we spoke with a Vice President of Sales who joined a company that was using our management model. He told us he had never in the past been able to get up to speed so quickly as he was at this organization. His team sat down with him. They showed him the scorecard, the meeting agenda and action register, and they showed him the non-negotiables that had been developed and agreed to by the leader of the team and the members of the team.

When Expectations Are Not Met

It's doubtful any Harveys would exist in a team constituted as the one we have described above. Charlie would set forth the problems confronting the team at a meeting, and if Harvey was selected to take action on one of them, his name would be placed on the action register with a due date. Surrounded by his teammates, peer pressure would likely compel him to agree to the assignment, and he would have to deliver or face them as an admitted slacker.

But suppose Harvey or another team member does fail to live up to the expectations of the team?

What should happen, for example, if an employee—Let's call him Harvey—typically works only three hours a day and spends the other four hours in the break room? Obviously, Harvey is not living up to expectations, which in this case is, "support your team members in everything they do."

If he has built his team properly, this should not be

Charlie, the team leader's problem. One of Harvey's team members should go to Harvey and tell him he isn't living up to the expectations of the team. By taking such long and frequent breaks, Harvey is violation of what he agreed to when he signed on. His slothful behavior creates more work for others because they have to take up the slack that comes about as a result of his absences.

Our experience has been that nine times out of ten this conversation will take care of the issue.

What should happen if a worker first goes to Charlie, the leader, about Harvey's behavior?

The leader should ask if the worker has had a conversation with Harvey. This team-member-to-team-member conversation needs to happen before any other action is taken.

Suppose the conversation is held, but Harvey continues taking long breaks?

The situation should be brought up at a team meeting, during the "around the table" agenda item. This can be done in one of two ways, depending on the maturity of the team. One would be to begin by not mentioning any names. So, if a team is new to the process, someone might say, "There is a member of our team who is working only about three hours a day and spending the rest of the time in the break room." David will now know he has now been put on notice and that the team leader is going to be looking out to see who is the guilty party.

On the other hand, in a mature team, someone might simply say, "Harvey is spending an inordinate amount of time in the break room and that's making more work for the rest of us." If this is indeed the case, others will certainly support this statement.

If the issue is not resolved once these steps have been taken and several weeks have passed, it is time for the team leader to get involved. This leads to the final topic we wish to cover in this chapter, which is individual performance management.

Performance Management

Do you dread doing performance appraisals? If you do, you are not alone. Most managers dread doing them because these managers do not have good data sources from which to draw information. Our system remedies this.

Most employees go into an appraisal with the assumption that if they have heard nothing, then they must be doing all right. Alternatively, some experience anxiety before a performance appraisal because they do not know what the appraisal is going to reflect. These situations exist because performance appraisals are typically a formal annual or semi-annual event in which the manager sits down with the employee and discusses past performance, with an eye to the future. We have found, however, that performance appraisals as stand-alone events such as this are not effective. What is effective, is performance management.

Performance management is an ongoing process. The manager maintains documentation and engages in ongoing dialogue with the employee in an effort to change work behaviors and outputs. The performance management process involves rewarding and acknowledging good performance, identifying and rectifying deficient performance and applying consequences to unchanged behavior and performance.

Our system allows leaders to collect the data necessary for continuous performance management. This is done through the meeting action register, where all the actions assigned to each individual and what happened as a result are documented.

We have found that in a mature team, about 80 percent of actions tie to scorecard items. The action register becomes an important historical record because an analysis of who has taken actions and how each individual has performed can provide an important indicator of the contribution of each team member. In other words, information from an action register can be rolled up periodically to give a clear picture of what the various members of the team are doing to advance the business. Such an analysis can be performed as frequently as needed to provide, for example, the data Charlie needs to coach Harvey and to manage his performance.

Chapter Nine
Non-Negotiable Systems and Processes

If something is said to be non-negotiable most people understand that to mean it is not open to discussion and must be done. Yet, in most companies and organizations, we come in contact with an unspoken belief that everything is negotiable. This has come about because of a desire to build innovative and creative organizations comprised of collaborative teams. Certainly, there must be some flexibility in order to improve and innovate, but a mistake too often made is to allow certain operational matters to become negotiable. Some must be non-negotiable, or situations will be created in which it is impossible to move beyond the three Ps.

To our way of thinking, four systems need to fall into the non-negotiable category. These systems should be the same throughout the organization—at every level and location, from Saigon to San José. They should not change based on who is leading the team, the seniority of the team or function of the team—variables that historically have been used to rationalize, explain and negotiate different methodologies.

Non-negotiables are not punitive. Some, when they hear "non-negotiable," immediately believe that something has been taken from them—they are being told what they cannot do. But we believe that most organizations, even those that are heavily unionized, want to work in an organization where good communication and clarity exist, where there is something to rally around that brings a sense of connectivity, where if someone moves from one department or location to another, they will find a similar way of operating and consistency. They are looking for and will warm to an organization that operates based on the three Cs—Clarity, Connectivity, and Consistency.

But the three Cs will not and cannot exist until certain things are determined and set by the leaders as non-negotiable—the processes by which the organization operates. As a leader, be prepared to stand firm because there may be some pushback against this. For example, one of our team recently returned from a workshop with Human Resource Directors from a number of top-level companies. Three of them pulled our colleague aside during the cocktail hour and said they would like to give him some feedback.

"We like what you had to say," they told him, "but we thought maybe if you would soften up the nomenclature—instead of saying non-negotiable processes, you said 'proven processes' or 'recommended processes'—it would go down better."

Our colleague realized these HR executives had missed the point of his presentation. They apparently believed the approached needed to be softened up in order to be salable, that there would be a greater likelihood of acceptance by the people in their organizations if it could be made to sound more palatable. What they did not realize is that most people in organizations today are hungry for leaders to lead—that they will actually welcome structure. Many in organizations today are victims of the lack of structure. Having something that is non-negotiable gives people something they can count on. They hunger for clarity and consistency. You might say they are looking for "freedom within fences."

Perhaps you have heard the story that follows, once told by a kindergarten teacher. A new school opened before a fence could be built around the playground. When the children went out to recess, they clustered close to the schoolhouse. Only a very few adventurous souls wandered out to the edges of the playground. It was simply much too scary for most to move away from the safety of what they saw as home base. After a fence went up, however, the situation changed. Almost immediately, the children became fairly evenly dispersed throughout the playground. Apparently, they felt a new sense of freedom—at liberty you might say to roam freely within the fence. The same can be true of people in an organization. Because they know where the boundaries are, the fences, they feel free to devote their full energy to work within those boundaries to accomplish the maximum possible. Without non-negotiable rules and systems, they might not know where to begin.

Systems Must Be Visible and Auditable

To move from managing by personality to managing by process, the processes must be visible and auditable.

Ideally, the non-negotiable processes will start at the top of the organization so that they encompass the entire organization. It should be possible to enter the organization at any level and see those processes in action and to validate that they are in place.

The senior team implementing these processes, no matter

where that team happens to be in the organization, must set the non-negotiables and practice them before they are rolled out.

Obviously, the lead team must practice what it preaches. If it cannot put its own processes into operation and live with them, why should anyone else throughout the organization be expected to do so? Since the processes must be visible and auditable, everyone will know how well they are working.

Our experience has been that if the leaders embrace the new processes and make them work, there will be no difficulty in getting the rest of the organization go along—even those that are unionized. When organizations are run by personalities instead of systems, typically confusion is created. We have found it to be a fact that most of the issues lower level people and teams have to deal with are created unintentionally by personalities at higher levels in the organization.

Non-Negotiable Systems Combine to Form a Process

Connectivity is created when it is readily apparent to everyone if they are winning or losing. Winning and losing, the business in other words, is the one thing everyone in an organization has in common and is what can bind them together. Scorecards are used to accomplish this.

Next comes a system to make people accountable. Accountability is created by a system that measures engagement in a way that makes accountability visible and personal.

A third system binds these first two together. It takes the scorecard and builds a battle rhythm of communication, a cascading conduit in which the meetings an organization has drive the business. Meetings should not be in addition to the business, but rather, enablers of the business.

And finally, a behavioral system needs to be put in place. This will clearly integrate an organization's people into the above systems so that a sense of ownership of them is created. This will become clear as each system is discussed in more detail in the pages that follow.

Chapter Ten
Creating Accountability

Is there a system or methodology in your organization to make accountability personal and visible? Does the organization delineate between responsibility and accountability? What is the role of the leader in building a team driven by collective accountability rather than selective engagement? How does the leader ensure accountability equity so the team is not unmotivated by a real or perceived disparity of engagement?

Performance is achieved when people are held accountable to act on the objectives that support the business. A key tool of The Martin Management Method that brings about visible accountability is the action register. The action register is a logical extension of the business scorecard, which in our system is constructed and deployed in a way that ensures employees focus on issues important to the success of the company. The action register brings about visible accountability and drives accountability throughout the organization. It does so by publicly documenting the assignment of tasks to specific individuals, dates for completion of tasks, and results.

When leaders implement this tool along with the business scorecard, they eliminate ignorance as an excuse for tasks not completed, and they eliminate personality from the focus of business.

Focus does not help a company a great deal unless it can be brought down to a level where that focus can stimulate and capitalize upon clear and visible, personal accountability. Let's

Action Register United Branding Technologies

Action to be taken	Responsible	Deadline	Date completed	Comments

look at systems and processes that can take an organization that is not performing up to its potential to one in which things are humming along in the direction its leaders would like it to go.

The Scorecard System

Most companies and organizations keep score. Metrics are developed, recorded and circulated, but most business people we talk with do not find them to be particularly helpful. In such cases the effort involved does not seem to be worth the benefit derived. We work hard to get the data, we run the data, build a report, and after all that energy and effort has been expended, we find we cannot really see anything that can help us improve our efficiency or way of working day-to-day.

The fundamental purpose of any scorecard system should be to tell us within five seconds of looking at it whether or not we are winning or losing.

As stated in the Goals section, a good scorecard should do three things. It should educate, facilitate and motivate. Many leaders of companies go straight to the numbers and miss what a good scorecard system should do or be. A good score-card system should be used, deployed and sustained.

A Scorecard System Should Educate

The first question to ask in evaluating a scorecard system is whether or not people understand it. Do they understand acronyms such as EBIT (Earnings Before Interest and Taxes)?

You may be surprised to learn that one of our team once had a manager ask him what "overhead" was and how he could impact it. This was a person in charge of a large department with a good deal of overhead. To head off any potential confusion or misunderstanding, one company we know of issues a glossary of terms and an explanation of scorecards usage to new employees when they join the company. We believe this makes good sense. It shows new employees what's important.

Consider this. When orienting new employees, how many companies brief them on their first day about scorecards and the metrics of the business? Not many, we suspect.

If whether or not the business is winning or losing is not one of the first things communicated to a new employee, what message is being sent? Unfortunately, that winning is not a priority—that what we are about is not us as a team, but rather you and me as individuals.

The fact is people coming into an organization usually would like to know if it is profitable and how it is doing. One highly successful company we know of uses the first two hours of orientation to educate new employees on scorecards. They begin with the company's global scorecard and follow with the scorecard of the new employee's business unit or department.

A Scorecard System Should Facilitate

We believe that meetings should be enablers of the business not additions to the business. Yet a lack of meeting effectiveness typically shows up in most company surveys. This will always be the case in our view until a scorecard is used to facilitate meetings.

After a lack of meeting effectiveness surfaced as a big issue in a survey, one company we know of posted a job for fifty people to become black belt certified meeting facilitators. Those selected were sent to a posh hotel in Scottsdale, Arizona, where they spent one month being certified. They then returned to the organization to help improve meeting facilitation across the organization.

In effect, the company built a meeting facilitation plan based on the three Ps. The people selected had to have presence—they had to be able to stand in front of the group and articulate and persuade them. It came down to using personality to try to fix a systemic problem. Instead of a team captain leading a meeting, an outside expert would be brought in with the effect that the team captain was no longer in charge.

Here is how meetings work at a company we believe conducts them in the right way. The meeting takes place on Monday mornings and is led by the CEO. Most attendees work in the home office and are physically present. Others who happen to work in remote locations are present via GoToMeeting online conferencing. At 9:45 a.m. in the meeting room, the company scorecard is projected on a screen and made available to those attending by computer. At just before 10 o'clock when the staff walks or tunes in, their eyes are drawn to a scorecard with about 15 items on it, perhaps three of which are red and the rest green.

Everyone knows the purpose of the meeting is not "team time." The purpose is to take care of business, i.e., to drive the business forward by identifying issues facing the company, finding solutions and making assignments to carry them out, and given that only three metrics are in the red, the participants can expect a relatively short and painless meeting.

All can also see that twelve of the fifteen metrics are green. They instantly know the company is winning.

The three red items will, of course, be discussed. No one will be allowed to leave the room until specific actions with names and deadline dates have been identified and agree to.

This is how a scorecard facilitates a meeting. It instantly shows what whether the team is winning or losing and it pinpoints what needs to be focused upon. This becomes the primary purpose of the meeting and neither time nor energy is wasted. In the absence of a scorecard, the purpose of a meeting is likely to become individual wants and needs. Personalities become the driving force.

A System to Motivate Behavior

Scorecards will not be translated from thermometers into thermostats until a robust action register is married to the scorecard. What's important about scorecards is what is done about the data.

It's human nature that when anyone is called upon to brief a senior level executive, he or she would certainly like to have something good to say. When this is not the case, and the news is bad, most of us will invariably want to move on quickly to explain what is being done to correct the situation. But most organizations do not use scorecards for this purpose. A scorecard may show a situation is not what it should be, or what management would like it to be, but the scorecard does not show how it will be corrected.

To overcome this, some managers keep action logs or meeting minutes to document actions to be taken, which have been decided upon in a meeting. Often, however, this simply doesn't work. Those who were to take action sometimes conveniently forget their assignment or firmly object that, as they look back, it wasn't clear to them they were responsible. They may add that with all the many items on their plate these days, they would not possibly have agreed to add the issue at hand—after which, to justify their inaction, they are very like to reel off a long list of the other things they have to do. This dissertation and the ensuing discussion will be a total waste of time because they have nothing to do with running the business and the ball will not be moved forward a single inch.

Action registers (see example on page 82) eliminate this. Action Registers are married to the scorecard. It becomes a standard agenda item during which action decisions are made and recorded, including the individual who commits to take the action as well as the date it is to be completed. Everyone on a team knows the action register will be reviewed at the next meeting, and they know that if they are not going have the action completed, it is incumbent on them to negotiate a new completion date before the meeting.

Semi-Annual Management Briefings

To motivate, there also needs to be a periodic scorecard reconciliation. If someone never has to brief others on performance *vis a vis* objectives, that person never really owns those objectives. On the other hand, if someone has to stand before a group and tell the story, what worked and what didn't, that person will own them. This is why we recommend that each team in an organization be compelled to brief a management team two levels up from it a minimum of twice a year, and in some cases more frequently.

There are a couple of ways this can be done. At one company with which we are familiar, a schedule is put together so that everyone on every team knows by the second week in January the two dates when they will have to brief senior management on their action register. This can work, but it may also create a negative behavioral consequence. It's human nature for the team to want to make the briefing as positive as possible. As a result, a good deal of activity may go on behind the scenes to make things look good at the times the briefings have been scheduled.

Perhaps a better and potentially more effective way is the approach taken by another company. In this organization, each team is made aware they will be required to brief senior management twice during the year, but they are not told the dates these briefings will occur. All they know is that on any given date on which they are having a meeting, the team leader may get a call letting him or her know senior management will be joining them that same day. This should not be a problem for the team or its leader if they have established a meeting rhythm and things are moving along as they should. The people we know who work this way like having senior management sit in because it gives them the opportunity to ask for additional resources when needed.

Scorecard reconciliation

As has been discussed, it's important that scorecards throughout the organization relate to and support each other.

To insure this, we believe senior management should take a careful look at all scorecards throughout the organization at least quarterly. All scorecards should be printed out and laid side by side for a close look. This will serve several purposes. It will mitigate the possible gaming of the system, and it will make sure the scorecards link to and support one another. This exercise will also provide an opportunity to judge whether objectives and accompanying metrics are at the right level. An example of how they can end up on the wrong level was given under the heading "Goal Creep" (pages 62-63) earlier in this book. Suffice it to say questions should be asked. For example, if a team is not achieving a goal in one area, is there another team somewhere that could be supporting that goal? Scorecards should not be allowed to become independent reporting system silos.

Chapter Eleven
Action Register Non-Negotiables

When a SMART objective measurement is in the red, the meeting action register is used to record and document the action remedy decided upon. This includes who has agreed to be responsible for taking the action and the date agreed upon for the action to be completed.

Ample time, usually the longest allotted to a single agenda item, should be spent at the end of each meeting to review agreed upon actions and for those who are to take the actions to acknowledge that they accept the assignments. In other words, what each action will consist of should be made crystal clear, and the persons accepting the assignments should clearly confirm they understand and agree to the assignment. In addition, specific dates need to be identified and recorded. In no case should they be left open to interpretation such as "TBD" or "ASAP"—even if it's not clear how long an action will take. Having a date sets a process in motion because a method should also be in place and understood by all for renegotiating action due dates if for any reason they cannot be met.

When such non-negotiable rules are in place, action registers become a vital component of an effective accountability system. Let's take a closer look.

When Due Dates Cannot Be Met

An action and the timeframe for its completion may have made sense at the time it was agreed upon. The person who agreed to carry it out may have believed he or she would be able to do what was called for without a problem. But things change, and sometimes a task is not what it at first appeared to be. Perhaps, the action isn't as easy to accomplish as he or she thought, or for some reason it cannot be completed in the time allowed.

What should happen, then? Let's look at the leadership team of a company that uses this system.

The team meets on Monday mornings at ten o'clock. An action register review is an important agenda item for this team. If someone is supposed to have an action completed but cannot, a non-negotiable rule is that the individual must renegotiate a new due date with the team leader by the close of business Friday. This brings about a couple of desirable results. For one, it causes people to look at the action register before the day of the meeting.

Let's say Sam is supposed to have something done by the meeting on Monday, but cannot. So, he goes to the team leader on Friday and explains the situation. The leader is likely to be gracious about it and to agree to a new due date because Sam has thought ahead, taken responsibility, and behaved in the way the team leader expects of his team members. But, what if Sam does not go to the leader on Friday?

When Sam starts making excuses in the meeting, the leader will show his displeasure. He might say, "Sam, I don't recall having a conversation with you about the fact you weren't going to have this done. You and I need to have a follow up conversation about this issue, later. You need to explain to me what isn't clear to you about the meaning of the words, non-negotiable. Now, let's move on."

The leader has taken an important action. If he or she does not say something like this and have the follow up meeting with Sam, she can expect as many as half the team to fail to have actions completed at next week's meeting. Not only does the leader need to be clear about this, the process for renegotiating a due date also needs to be clear. Doing so with an email should not be an option. A conversation either in person or by telephone must take place and the leader must affirm the new due date. This means the owner of a pending action for which the due date needs to be renegotiated should not wait until Friday afternoon to begin trying to get in touch with the leader.

When it becomes clear to everyone that non-negotiables are just that, that rules are rules and action registers are serious business, meetings will begin to move along quickly. They will cease to be drawn out affairs because the focus will be on the business and the related actions needed or taken. A person will give his or her report, and attention will move to the next agenda item. Extraneous discussion will not be necessary. If a scorecard meeting is run right and contains a manageable number of red metrics, it should only last anywhere from 45 minutes to an hour.

Who Should Keep the Action Register

Every team needs to have a person assigned who keeps the action register in meetings. This role can rotate, but the role itself must be a dedicated one, and it should be performed in real time. This means the actions, persons responsible, and due dates should be recorded on the action register in the team meeting at the time they are decided upon. Ideally, the action register will be projected on a screen so that no mistake can be made about what is being recorded.

It is also important that only one centralized and universally accessible action register exist—either a hard copy in the team handbook or electronically in the handbook on a server—and that this be kept current at all times. An action register is an important way to create visibility so anyone who needs the information should have access to it at all times. Software tools are available for this, or a linked Excel spreadsheet can be used. When a due date is renegotiated, for example, the one who renegotiated the date should go into the system, change the date in the comments section and note who agreed to the change and when.

Unless a centralized action register exists, inconsistent records will most certainly come about and leaders and others will not have access to the most current information.

Accountability Analysis

Periodically, information from an action register can be rolled up to give a clear picture of what the various members of the team are doing to advance the business. Such an analysis might be performed quarterly, using the centralized action register database. As stated before, for a mature team about 80 percent of actions tie to scorecard items, which is to say this analysis is an important indicator of the contribution of each team member.

Chapter Twelve
Communications, the Foundational System

For any company or organization to achieve its performance potential, it must have a system in place for communicating that gets everyone on the same page and pulling together.

How does your organization do this? Is a communications system in place to drive a sense of urgency? Is there a cascading waterfall, or a battle rhythm of communication, that replicates on a regular schedule? Has the organization become dependent on technology to drive communication? Is what we call "advertising" the primary vehicle to drive messages?

Communication is a two-way street. We have seen that in top performing organizations, communication is not a random event, but rather, it is a planned process—just as is the case with any other business function. When planning a communication strategy, it is important to incorporate key elements that bring focus to meetings rather than endless discussion, enable participation, and provide a consistent flow of information.

Frequency: Since meetings tend to be the primary two-way communication vehicle in most organizations, a minimum frequency should be established for meetings of particular groups based on business cycles and needs. A team should meet at this minimum frequency to ensure timely communication with its members.

Purpose: It's important to define in advance the business purpose and outcomes desired from a particular meeting.

Specifying the purpose and outcomes enables focused preparation and clarity around topics, and it defines the level of urgency for activities that result from the meeting.

An Agenda: Every meeting ought to be planned around a standard agenda, which not only lists the topics to be discussed, but also the time frames in which to discuss them and the person who will lead a discussion or give a presentation. A structured agenda reinforces the business focus and sense of urgency for communication and action relative to the business topics. The agenda ought to include a status update of outstanding actions from the previous meeting as well as a verification of new actions that arise during the meeting so there is complete clarity about who is doing what and when.

Standard Meeting Agenda

- Action Register Review (5 min)
- Scorecard Review (15 min)
- Around the Table (5 min)
- Recognition (5 min)
- Pass up, Pass down ((5 min)
- Action Register Review (20 min)
- Meeting Audit (5 min)

Defined Roles: Meetings need a leader, a recorder and a timekeeper. These roles ought to be identified and filled prior to the meeting so that individuals come prepared to fulfill them. Filling these roles insures someone is ready to facilitate the agenda, document actions, capture information and document decisions.

Rules: There ought to be ground rules that define acceptable and unacceptable behavior in meetings. Some examples: no interruptions, be on time, respect one another, stay on the topic, everyone participates and cell phones off.

An Audit Process: A process should be in place that monitors and provides a basis for improving communication. One way is simply to ask the end of each meeting, "What went well during this meeting?" and "What needs to be done to improve the next meeting?"

It's important to keep in mind that communication only occurs face-to-face. Any other communication is advertising. Advertising can reinforce and supplement face-to-face communication but it should never be expected to replace it.

Clarity System

We have talked about scorecards, and we have talked about action registers. How does it all fit together? How is a battle rhythm created? The communications system is the key. It must be built and implemented based on how the process needs to be replicated. To illustrate this, let's return to a meeting of the leadership team that meets on Monday at ten o'clock.

When the team walked into the meeting, the scorecard was on the screen. Then, a meeting agenda such as the one shown above is put up. The first item is the Action Register review.

How long should this review take?

Only those items due on that day need to be reviewed. If an item that was due is not completed, it should have been renegotiated. So the time spent on this item should be short.

Next the Scorecard is on the list. Unless items have been green for 90 days or more, only red items and potential solutions will be discussed. The actions to be taken will be captured and recorded under the agenda item, Action Register Review.

This brings the meeting to "Around the Table." This should not lead to a dissertation on the part of each individual of what they do each week. Rather, it should be a 30 to 60 second opportunity to bring up an issue and get it on the action register, or to call attention to something the group needs to be aware of such as the pending visit of an important customer.

Recognition is next. A company will almost always benefit from institutionalizing recognition as a weekly discussion point. Some are uncomfortable with this because it seems to them to be forced. Even so, we suggest putting it on the agenda as a non-negotiable item because if recognition is not institutionalized, our experience has been that it probably won't happen.

Let's take a look at how this might work. The agenda at our example company cascades throughout the organization. Each member of the leadership team heads up his or her own team that meets weekly. Members of these teams head their own teams, and so on throughout the company. This enables recognition at the lowest level team to be passed up from team to team until it reaches the very top. When the top team reaches this item on the agenda, the person assigned to coordinate recognition gives his or her report.

The person might say, "This week we had eight recognitions that came up to us. Here they are. Hannah on the third shift at our plant in Walla Walla did such and such, John in

Peoria did so and so . . . " and so on.

Each recognition is then given out to a senior executive in the room to follow up. Over the next seven days, these senior executives will make contact with the person they were assigned. If the he or she will be in the office or plant where the person works, he will visit that person and speak to him personally.

If a face-to-face visit isn't possible, she might call the individual on the telephone and say something such as, "Hello Gloria, this is Hillary Starling, VP of Sales. I want you to know that we talked about what you did for the company at our executive committee meeting earlier this week. We want you to know that your action was spot on, and we sincerely appreciate your quick thinking. . . ."

The leaders of this company are making visible actions that benefit the company in a way that can literally transform behavior throughout the organization—literally lift it to a new and higher level. We submit that if a mechanism to make this happen is not in place, it will happen only sporadically or not at all.

Pass Up, Pass Down

As we alluded to earlier, there is a big difference between advertising and communicating. Many organizations have mastered advertising. Because of this, the leaders of these organizations have falsely convinced themselves they are communicating when they are not communicating.

Anyone who has a teenager in the house or has been a teenager not so long ago will understand why we say this. When one reaches the age of sixteen, gets a driver's license and wants to start going out with friends, most parents will give that young person a curfew. So think back. When your mom and dad gave you a curfew, did they write it on a note, side it under your bedroom door and say, "Honey, when you get a chance, give us some feedback."

We doubt it.

Usually, people tell us this message was delivered face to face, and it was not delivered only once. When many of us left the house, one of our parents would say, "When will you be home?" This wasn't really a question. The parent was seeking validation that the message had been given and received.

Why was this important?

Once that verbal affirmation occurred, the teenager could be held accountable.

As stated above, most leaders of companies think they are communicating to their employees and when they are in actually advertising. Newsletters, bulletin boards, emails blasts and the like are much like sliding a note under a teenager's bedroom door. They do not require people to engage. But suppose they do get the message? If what we are attempting to communicate is not to their liking, such as a 11 p.m. curfew, they may feign ignorance.

The pass up, pass down system can be beneficial in big ways and small. One of our team once got a call from a friend at another company who said people in suits were walking around in the building where he worked. Naturally, the friend wondered if his company was being sold. The rumor mill was already in high gear. It turned out that the people in suits were from a company that had just become a new customer and were on an orientation tour. The rumors could easily have been avoided if the fact that the tour was going to take place had been brought up during the pass up, pass down agenda item.

Another company we know of with about 8000 employees changed its health care package. What had been a generous package became less generous. Historically, a change in benefits had been communicated by this company through a letter and an information packet sent to employees' homes, and of course, the information was also posted on bulletin boards throughout the company. This time, however, leadership decided to do it differently because they now had a past-down process in place. This was possible because everyone in the company was on a team and each came together once a week in a meeting. It started with the top leadership team in the company, which met on Monday mornings at 10 o'clock.

This company's pass down process used bullet points, which are the key points leadership wants everyone to know during a communications cycle. The pass down is agreed upon in the leadership team's Monday morning meeting.

This particular pass down went something like this:

Our health care benefits are changing. We are going from Blue Cross, Blue Shield to such and such a provider. We are going from a co-pay of $20 to a co-pay of $40. We are going from a family deductible of $100 to $1000.

These points were approved in the 10 a.m. Monday morning meeting. At one o'clock on Monday, the vice presidents had their team meetings and verbally delivered the pass downs. At three o'clock Monday afternoon those who had met with a vice president had their meetings and verbally delivered the pass downs, and on it went until by Thursday afternoon, everyone in the company should have been informed about the change in benefits in a meeting—all of which, by the way, included a scorecard and an action register.

Sometimes the president of this company stands next to a time clock in one of the company's plants and asks questions of those punching out.

He might say, "Excuse me, can you tell me one of the pass down items in your meeting this week?"

The reply he might get could be something like, "Yes, our health care benefit are being cut. The co-pay is going to double and the deductible is going through the roof."

Although he may not like the way this employee feels, his question has validated that she got the message.

Suppose, however, he asks the question and the person has no idea what was in the pass down?

He will ask the person if the weekly scorecard meeting took place. If the person says no, the next question will be, "Who is your team leader?"

Because the leader of the company does this, people take the system seriously and it works.

The Meeting Audit

You will probably not be surprised to hear that most companies have too many meetings. The truth is many seem to be in a cycle of meetings they seem to be unable to break. No wonder we hear so many complaints about meetings—everything from those that are a total waste of time because the discussions amount to little more than gripe sessions, to those that at least accomplished something but could have lasted fifteen minutes instead of half the day—if the leader had just kept people from wandering off topic.

Meeting audits are a way to cut down on unproductive meeting time spent. We recommend that no meeting should end until the following question is answered by everyone in attendance: "Was this meeting an enabler of our business, or was it in addition to the business?"

The leader should go around the table and have everyone in attendance express his or her opinion in the spirit of, "If the meeting wasn't as good and productive today as it might have been, what can we do next time to make it better?"

Weekly scorecard review meetings typically should not last more than an hour. In one company we know, the average manager spent 23 hours a week in meetings before our system was instituted. The 23-hour figure was cut to only five once it was in place and working as intended. Two of those five hours now are typically spent in two meetings: the meeting he or she attends with his boss and peers and the one he leads with his subordinates. The other three hours are spent in meetings that support special projects, committees meetings, and so forth.

Cutting Down on Meetings

The Martin Method is meant to build a battle rhythm so that a pattern is built that moves the business forward. As this rhythm takes hold, an overall effort can be undertaken to align and streamline the company's meetings. The system should provide the basic information to run the business. Many meetings companies have are an outgrowth of not having the information they need. Meetings then spring up to deal with the lack of information. Once the system is in place and mature, it should be possible to make a list of all the meetings that take place and decide how that list can be modified and streamlined. Which meetings can be eliminated? Which can be cut from weekly to monthly or from monthly to quarterly?

Chapter Thirteen
The Behavioral System

As was mentioned earlier, it's important to for the members of a team to discuss and agree upon how they will work together. The leader and his or her team members need to put down on paper what they expect of each other. They should do so in measurable terms, and they should sign off on them.

In the People section, we also detailed a three-step process for use when expectations are not being met by a team member. First a fellow team member should have a private chat with the offender. If that does not resolve the issue, it should be brought before the entire team at a regular meeting during Around-The-Table. Finally, if these initiatives fail, the team leader will have to get involved. This and other agree-upon procedures should be clearly stated in a team handbook.

A Team Handbook Contains:
- Procedures
- Non-negotiables and team expectations
- Contact information for each team member
- An up-to-date scorecard and action register
- Historical scorecard and action register data

A team handbook is the nexus of the Martin Management Method. For a small outfit, this is a three-ring binder kept in a central location. Software can be purchased that a large organization can use to create an electronic handbook to be kept on a central server. Regardless of the form it takes, a handbook should be available to anyone who needs to refer to it. Moreover, it should contain everything to do with the team, including agreed-upon procedures, non-negotiables and team expectations, contact information for each team member, an up-to-date scorecard and action register, and historical information and data.

The handbook gives order and consistency to the team's business by outlining its purpose and processes and serving as a public record of its work. Teams use handbooks to orient new team members and to train them in team procedures and job responsibilities, as well as to reinforce non-negotiables and to audit team processes.

Because it is available to anyone who may need to refer to it, the team handbook removes ignorance as an excuse, and it elevates expectations by holding everyone accountable. Along with action registers, a team handbook documents expectations for behavior, and it provides a mechanism for team leaders to be consistent.

Large companies will benefit from having a fully integrated software system that ties team handbooks together throughout the organization. Such software is available off the shelf. It should be Internet based so it can be accessed from anywhere in the world via a permission-based login procedure. Moreover, different employees can be allowed different levels of access depending on their needs.

The software allows scorecards to be customized to meet the specific needs of different users and populated manually in the same manner as an Excel spreadsheet. Data can also be imported from a CSV [Comma Separated Values] file or directly from an ERP [Enterprise Resource Planning] system.

Someone with full access to the entire the data base of a company, such as a CEO, can roll up information on a historical basis to determine trends, look at what is going on with a single team at any given time, past or present, or slice and dice the data in a myriad of ways that will provide an abundance of information he or she can use to run the business. For example, the leader can quickly review scorecards from each team. Because progress toward SMART Objectives are color coded, how each team is performing can be seen at a glance. Past and present data is there, so trends can be spotted easily. Action registers are linked to each scorecard, so the leader can see what corrective action plans are in place and being implemented, as well as when a resolution is due. Moreover, a built-in audit system offered by the software provider allows changes to be tracked, including due dates and the personnel responsible. This make it possible for leaders to follow up quickly on problem areas and to enable or empower those assigned to the task to get it done. It also facilitates the recognition of employees for their accomplishments.

Chapter Fourteen
Where Do You Stand as a Leader?

No matter how good or how effective a management process may be, it will always benefit and prove even more effective if it is run by a leader who commands the respect and admiration of those individuals he or she leads. With this in mind, we ask you to consider what your people would say about you as a leader.

When was the last time you asked them how you were doing? Creating a culture of candor and transparency regardless of relationship is a key pillar for effective leaders, but there are other attributes possessed by effective leaders as well. As we move through a discussion of them, we suggest you consider how you measure up.

Humility Tops the List

Humility, which is the acknowledgment of who we are in relation to others, is essential to effective leadership. A leader secure enough to admit he or she does not have, or need to have, all the answers is typically rewarded with loyal followers. A leader whose focus is on him or herself, and how much he knows or is capable of doing alone, lacks empathy—the ability to stand in another's shoes—and that usually rubs people the wrong way.

Most successful leaders are confident, of course. Often, their confidence is an outgrowth of the passion and commitment they feel to their cause. The leader believes change will happen through persistence, hard work, and knowing he or she has the right system and is doing the right thing. In this way, the cause becomes bigger than the leader. Arrogant leaders, on the other hand, believe they are greater than the cause. People are drawn to leaders who appear confident and effective, but they warm to and give lasting support to those who combine self-confidence with humility.

Giving Credit to Others Also Builds Loyalty

Here's another area for self-evaluation that's related to humility. Rather than take credit for achievements, great leaders build loyalty on top of trust by giving credit where credit is due—and perhaps sometimes even when it is not. Where do you stand in this regard?

Whether you are liberal or conservative politically, you will have to admit that many people believe Ronald Reagan was one of the great leaders of the twentieth century. Consider how Reagan almost never took credit for the achievements of his administration, but instead was quick to praise his staff. In doing so he achieved a high level of loyalty among his followers.

Few have said it better than legendary Alabama football coach, Paul "Bear" Bryant, "If anything goes bad, I did it. If anything goes semi-good, we did it. If anything goes really good, then you did it. That's all it takes to get people to win football games for you."

What else is a great leader able to do? He or she is able to articulate a vision the team can easily grasp. For Reagan it was his "Shining City on a Hill." The leader points the way for the team to proceed to realization of the vision and in doing so generates optimism and bolsters belief the goal can be reached. We all know how powerful and self-fulfilling the belief can be that a particular outcome is inevitable.

Other Qualities of Great Leaders

Are you a good listener? Do you really stop and take time to hear and understand what those under your supervision are trying to tell you?

Great leaders are almost always good listeners. They want to know what others think, and do not believe they, themselves, always have the best or right answer. They are smart enough to use the intelligence and the experience of others, and understand a good idea can come from anywhere, at any time, and from anyone. When a great leader comes in contact with an idea that makes sense, he or she recognizes and heeds the sensation of truth that resonates within. You might say the idea or thought seems to "click." Timid or unsure individuals often will dismiss this feeling. Great leaders are secure with themselves. They see when someone else has a better idea, and they have the self-confidence to put that idea to work.

Great leaders have and show respect for the people they lead, whether they are soldiers, employees, players, or citizens. They lead by example and by doing so demonstrate they are worthy of being followed. They are personally committed to the institution they lead, as well as the objective of the institution, and are out front personally doing whatever they can to reach it.

Leading by Example

For everyone to pull together for success, leaders need to

roll up their sleeves and get their hands dirty right next to their employees. The goal is for everyone to feel a sense of equality, that they are members of the same team regardless of the titles that follow their names. Employees are not blind. They see what is going on. They watch executives closely and determine for themselves if each one is "walking the talk." Employees quickly figure out which leaders are personally committed and which are not. They know which ones are only looking out for number one, and they respond to and follow the leaders accordingly.

That's why it is important to focus on building a team, not individual stars. And as the team leader, your primary job is to serve the team, to facilitate, to clear the path so that the team can make what needs to happen, happen—in order to reach the goal. As a great leader of long ago once said, "Whoever wants to be great among you must be your servant, and whoever wants to be first must be the servant of all." In other words, you do not get to be and stay the leader by serving yourself and having others serve you. People follow because ultimately you are serving them.

HAVING EVALUATED yourself based on what has been said in this chapter, we would be surprised if you did not find areas that need improvement. Seeing yourself and others in a new light is the first step. It is something that would be of benefit to most people. Rather than thinking of ourselves as supervisors or line operators, for example, we might improve by seeing ourselves as coaches or key players on a team. Rather than regarding others as co-workers or subordinates, we must come to view them as fellow team members.

Perhaps you have conducted an honest evaluation of your-self and have identified some things to work on. How can you go about a personal transformation? Some may think this is impossible. "I was born this way. I can't be somebody I'm not," will be the position they take. They are wrong. Anyone can change. In fact, the happiest seem to do so readily.

In his book, *The Seven Habits of Highly Effective People,* Stephen Covey writes about a realization that altered his life. He was wandering among stacks of books in a college library when he came across one that drew his interest. He opened it, and was so moved by what he read that he reread the para-graph many times. It contained the simple idea that a gap exists between stimulus and response, and that the key to growth and happiness is how this gap is used. People have the power to *choose* in that fraction of a second. They can choose to help a coworker—when yesterday they may ignored the opportunity. They can choose to pass when the dessert cart comes by, and skip the calories.

Richard Carlson, the author of *Don't Sweat the Small Stuff . . . and It's All Small Stuff,* picks up on the same idea. His advice is always to take a breath before speaking or taking action. If you adopt this, you will rid yourself of the habit of reacting in a repetitive way. You will begin taking a consid-ered approach, and taking a considered approach can lead to all sorts of good things such as better relationships with friends, family, and co-workers.

Another way is to become what some have called a "silent observer" of yourself. The idea is to move your point of view out of your head, and place it on your shoulder or the ceiling. Then watch yourself go about your business. Once you start keeping an eye out, you may see things that are not helping you get where you want to go. Once you see what is diverting you from your desired destination, it is but a short step to self-transformation.

Generational Awareness Helps Leaders Lead

When it comes to leading people, it helps to understand their perspective and worldview. Every individual is different, of course, but some helpful insight often can come from considering the general characteristics of the generation a person was born into. Today, four distinct groups can be found in the workforce. The oldest, known as Traditionalists or Matures, was born before 1946. At this point in their careers they tend to identify with building a legacy at work and believe that no news is good news when it comes to their performance. Most are actively planning for retirement.

Traditionalists / Matures

• Born before 1946

• No News Is Good News

• Are Planning Retirement

• Would Like to Leave a Legacy

Baby Boomers are next. There are approximately 76 million in the workforce, born from 1946 through 1964. Much has been written about this large cohort, which has been compared to a pig in a python because of its sheer size compared to the generations that preceded and immediately followed it.

Boomers tend to focus on building their careers, prefer to work regular hours but usually do not complain when they have to stay to get a job done. They want to know how things are going with respect to their personal performance and at minimum expect annual feedback with ample documentation. Only after they feel they have their jobs well under control do they begin to devote time and energy on finding personal meaning.

Baby Boomers

- Born 1946-1964

- Careers Come First

- Programmed to Get the Job Done

- Want and Expect Feedback

The generation that follows, born between 1965 and 1976 and known as Generation X, is different. Its members tend to want portable careers and need feedback, but hesitate to ask for it, so it is best to keep an open dialog going with them if you want them to stay on board. Growing up, many saw their parents laid off or face job insecurity. As a result, they frequently have a different view of loyalty than Boomers or Matures. Rather than their company or place of employment, they are more likely to have a commitment to their work, to the team they work with, and to the boss they work for.

A Boomer might complain about his dissatisfaction with management, but simply shrug it off as something that comes with the job. A Gen Xer, on the other hand, will be less likely to waste time complaining. More likely, he or she will update and send out a resume, and accept the best offer that comes along. Unlike Boomers who tend to prefer a retirement plan with benefits, it is not surprising that Gen Xers would usually rather have a portable 401K with lump sum distribution.

Generation X

- Born 1965-1976

- Want Portable Careers

- Saw Parents Struggle in Hard Economic Times

- Loyal to People, Not Companies

- Quick to Change Jobs When Dissatisfied

- Want Feedback but Hesitate to Ask for It

Bringing up the rear is the 75 million strong Generation Y, also known as the Millennial Generation, born between 1977 and 1998—which happens to have been the most child-centric time in our nation's history. Perhaps because of the doting attention they received and the high expectations of their parents, they tend to display a great deal of self-confidence and may even appear cocky. As you might expect, this group is technologically highly literate. After all, technology has always been part of their lives, whether it has to do with the Internet,

Internet, social media, iPads, iPhones, iPods, or whatever gadget has just been released.

Millennials are typically team-oriented, having banded together to date and socialize rather than pairing off. They work well in groups, preferring this to solitary endeavors, and are good multi-taskers—because they were programmed wall-to-wall by parents and grew up juggling sports, school, church activities and social interests—with the result that they can be expected to work hard and get jobs done.

Generation Y / Millennials

- Born 1977-1998

- Had Helicopter Parents

- High Level of Self-Confidence

- May Lack Tact and Social Graces

- Team Oriented

- Multi-Taskers

- Technologically Savvy

- Seek Relationships at All Levels

- Want and Expect Frequent Feedback

Millennials seem to expect structure in the workplace—they acknowledge and respect positions and titles, and want a relationship with their boss—but they approach work from a different perspective than the older generations. They want to build parallel careers with flexibility to balance "the other things" in their lives. They also want feedback at the push of a button and, while they usually present themselves as affable and courteous, can be a challenge to manage and lead because they have high expectations of themselves and their employers.

Millennials want to keep learning—being bored is a reason to find a new job. As a result, they do not mind leaving a job after less than a year, especially if they think leaders are not listening to them. They often believe they know the best way to do something and will tell you when they do. Hierarchy does not matter much to them—they want to have relationships with everyone. Often, however, they were not taught proper social skills and do not treat older employees as some may think they should.

Millennials usually possess a need to understand the goal and why a policy is in place. They want to do things their way, so it may be wise to let them create the process. They also need to know what the values and vision is for their work.

Chapter Fifteen
Time to Get to Work

Matures and Baby Boomers may remember a television show that aired from 1952 to 1975 called "Death Valley Days." Ronald Reagan acted in a few episodes and was its host during 1964 and 1965.

The show was sponsored primarily by the Pacific Coast Borax Company, which advertised a product called "20 Mule Team Borax," a brand of household cleaner. The product was named for the twenty-mule teams that were used in the years between 1883 and 1889 to haul borax by wagon out of Death Valley, California, to the nearest rail spur. Twenty mules pulling a wagon were often pictured during the opening and closing credits. It was an impressive sight.

Imagine harnessing twenty mules and getting them all headed in the right direction, pulling together. That would seem a monumental task—almost as difficult as harnessing all the people in your organization and getting them to pull together in unison. No one would expect that to be easy, whether those for whom you are responsible number less than a dozen or in the tens of thousands. But now it can be done, and if we have accomplished the job we set out to do, this book has explained how.

The Legacy of a Leader

Recently one of us went to the retirement dinner held for a senior executive of a client company. It was a very nice affair. People said many positive things about him, and he received a gold watch. But the legacy this man left was much less, we are certain, than he had hoped. You see, by the first Friday after his retirement, his team was in total disarray.

During a period of decades, this executive had assumed roles that should have remained with members of his staff. Over time, he had come to know their individual strengths and their individual weaknesses, and though he relied on their strengths, he compensated for their weaknesses by performing functions they should have been performing for themselves.

Predictably, this became the expectation on the part of those whose weaknesses he shored up, so that after his retirement, a number of things he had routinely taken care of simply did not get done. Not until after he was gone did the full scope of what he had been doing for his team become visible.

We have seen similar situations many times. Often we are called upon help because the performance of an organization that once was going well has deteriorated significantly. The first question we ask in such a circumstance is whether any management or organizational changes have recently taken place. The answer is usually that there has indeed been a re-organization, or that a key individual has left. In these cases, what had been holding the organization together was not processes and systems, it was personalities.

We have made many references to the three Ps. It bears repeating that a major problem they create is an unsustainable situation. Take one person out of the mix and a whole organization can crumble because the glue that was holding everything together was not a system, not a process, it was the sheer will, determination and attributes of a key individual.

While the three Ps can drive performance, we believe that as leaders we are obligated to adopt a process that will sustain performance—whether or not we are present. A battle rhythm of systems needs to be put in place so that if and when the current leader leaves and someone else steps in, a seamless transition will take place.

Managing by personality is one of the pitfalls many companies and organizations have fallen into as a result of downsizing and moving to empowered teams. All the touchy-feely leadership advice of the last decade has not served well those who must lead others. Dictating can be counterproductive, too, of course, just as touchy-feeling is not the way to get an organization moving ahead.

The Martin Management Method is the way. Scorecards and action registers insure leaders do not subconsciously play favorites. They force everyone to accept accountability. Each person must pull his or her own weight or be exposed to peers. And, as any parent of a teenager knows, peer pressure can be powerful.

One thing is certain. Team leaders can easily end up doing all the team's work if they do not have such system in place. The economic downturn that began in late 2007 and the austerity-based thinking that came about as a result have created numerous situations in which leaders have more responsibility than they can handle effectively, assuming they continue to operate in the old, traditional way. Often, open positions have not been filled—leaving those leaders who remain with more roles and tasks to execute. Our system offers a way not only to compensate, but to excel in situations such as this.

Let us ask you this. If you left your organization today, what would be your leadership legacy? Have you been relying on the three P's? If so, you may be able to accomplish what you must. You may be getting done the tasks and activities that absolutely have to be done in order to drive the business forward. But ask yourself, are you creating and maintaining a culture of dependency? Are your team members like our colleague's boys we wrote about, waiting in the garage, twiddling their thumbs, about to blow the horn because you are not moving fast enough to suit them?

If so, you may have created a situation in which you have become paramount to the organization's success, and of course, that may be rewarding in a way. But an unintended consequence may be a life that is less fulfilling outside of work than it otherwise might be—a hectic life in which free time, time to think and reflect, comes at a very high premium.

One thing is absolutely certain if this is true. The situation you have created is unsustainable. The time has come to change it, don't you agree?

Use this book. Or, give us a call. We'd like to help.